*"How to" guide*

# Promoting your Cause

## A guide for fundraisers and campaigners

**Karen Gilchrist**

DIRECTORY OF SOCIAL CHANGE

CAF

Published by
The Directory of Social Change
24 Stephenson Way
London NW1 2DP
Tel: 020 7209 5151, fax: 020 7391 4804
e-mail: info@dsc.org.uk
from whom further copies and a full publications list are available.

The Directory of Social Change is a Registered Charity no. 800517

First published 2002

ISBN 1 900360 95  0

**British Library Cataloguing in Publication Data**
A catalogue record for this book is available from the British Library

Cover design by Lenn Darroux
Text designed by Sarah Nicholson
Typeset, printed and bound by Stephen Austin, Hertford.

Other Directory of Social Change departments in London:
Courses and conferences tel: 020 7209 4949
Charityfair/Charity Centre tel: 020 7209 1015
Publicity tel: 020 7391 4900
Research tel: 020 7391 4880

Directory of Social Change Northern Office:
Federation House, Hope Street, Liverpool L1 9BW
Courses and conferences tel: 0151 708 0117
Research tel: 0151 708 0136

# Contents

ABOUT THE AUTHOR                                                                    iv

INTRODUCTION                                                                        1

CHAPTER 1        What promotional techniques can help?                              5

CHAPTER 2        Your identity                                                      8

CHAPTER 3        Printed material                                                   24

CHAPTER 4        Websites                                                           40

CHAPTER 5        Video and audio                                                    48

CHAPTER 6        Using the media                                                    56

CHAPTER 7        Open days, roadshows, balls, conferences
                 and exhibitions                                                    76

CHAPTER 8        Making a presentation                                             85

CHAPTER 9        Merchandise                                                        96

CHAPTER 10       Creative packages                                                 101

CHAPTER 11       Finishing touches                                                 105

CHAPTER 12       Finding out how you are doing                                     107

FURTHER INFORMATION                                                                110

# About the author

Karen Gilchrist is a director of a communications company called Resource Base. The organisation has a special interest in social affairs, education, health, personal development and creativity. She is a writer, researcher and producer, working on community programmes for regional television, producing health and social care videos and implementing media relations for a number of grant-makers in the south east region. She is a trustee of Community Action Hampshire.

# Introduction

This book has been written for people who raise funds for charities and community organisations and for those campaigning on the group's behalf. It does not tell you how to raise your group's income directly, but it does contain ideas on how to raise the profile of your organisation, establish a positive reputation, increase awareness of your work or cause, and communicate effectively with your target audiences. All these things should make your organisation's fundraising work just a bit easier and, crucially, they should help you to get your messages across – helping to change people's minds and behaviour.

This book is for anyone who is raising funds for, or campaigning on behalf of, a voluntary organisation. That might mean someone with the job title 'fundraiser' or 'campaigner', but could equally mean an organisation's director or chief executive, volunteer or trustee taking on a particular role for the group. It would also be helpful for anyone running a discrete project within an organisation, where the project manager is expected to wear a number of hats, including that of promoting the project to a range of audiences.

## How this book can help fundraisers

As a fundraiser you have to speak to a wide range of different people in different roles. You need to introduce your organisation to different types of potential donor: individuals, corporations, trusts and foundations, statutory bodies and others. All have different motivations for giving and will respond to different styles of approach and messages. If they have never heard of your group before, though, you have a lot of convincing to do in a limited amount of time.

If potential funders have already heard of your group, think it is doing a good job and realise the significance of your work, then they will be more receptive to appeals for support. On occasion they might even approach you, offering money or inviting you to work in partnership with them.

Once people have been convinced and have given money to your organisation there is still a need for effective and professional communication. Funders need to be thanked, kept informed and possibly asked (tactfully) for more. They may have to justify their decision to support your group to shareholders, members, the Charity Commission or voters, and you need to report to them in an appropriate way.

Furthermore, some funders may invest in your work and attach particular conditions to their support, again requiring excellent communication and promotional skills. As a grant recipient or project partner you could be called on to make a presentation to a national conference, write an article for an annual report or attract media coverage for a sponsorship, for example.

You might also want to make the most of other promotional techniques in your fundraising work, for example producing a video to show a good piece of work that needs to develop with further funding, creating a website to host an online auction, or creating merchandise to raise your organisation's profile and some income.

Fundraisers are required to do much more than write a convincing letter asking for money. You need to be able to communicate in numerous ways, always presenting your organisation in the most appropriate and favourable way. This book aims to help you do just that.

## How this book can help campaigners

People who campaign on behalf of a cause generally feel strongly, often passionately, about it. Their energy, expertise and commitment can attract attention from the media, public and politicians. But an individual, however fired up and charismatic, cannot be everywhere. If you are to campaign effectively you need your messages to be supported, reinforced and spread more widely. This can be achieved through promotional materials, media coverage, and colleagues. The techniques outlined in this book should help you to ensure the messages conveyed by you and others support and enhance your campaigning work.

# How this book can help project managers

When you are running your own project within a voluntary organisation you take on a number of different roles. Not only are you planning, budgeting, and coordinating the work, you also promote it to a range of target audiences. Sometimes the project is closely associated with your 'host' organisation, sometimes it has a very clear separate identity. In the latter case you are in a position of almost running your own small organisation and everything in this book that applies in a larger sense to whole charities could apply to your individual project.

# How you might use this book

There are a number of topics covered in this guide, and few fundraisers or campaigners would have the budget, need and authority to work on all areas at once. However, we have tried to come up with a handy reference book so that when the time comes to commission a website or produce a schools resource pack, for instance, you have some helpful hints on the shelf. When you need to develop a newsletter or exhibition panels, you will have a checklist to refer to, and should you be called on to revamp the organisation's corporate identity you have some guidelines to work to.

# What promotional techniques can help?

**I**n this brief chapter we give you an overview of the different topics covered in the book. You will find out what areas are included and why they are of value to fundraisers and campaigners.

**The key points covered are:**

▶ why fundraisers and campaigners have to be experts at communicating;
▶ the promotional tools covered in this book.

## Why you need to be an expert communicator

When you care deeply about a particular cause it is easy to slip into jargon and make assumptions about how much others understand about the need for your organisation and the type of work you do. This can be reinforced by the group of people who are naturally attracted to support an organisation's work as volunteers or trustees. They will be drawn to the cause because they share your concerns. But once you look outside that group of people, you need to explain things simply, justifying the need for your work, and describing clearly what you are trying to do, as well as outlining what support can help you achieve this.

So fundraisers and campaigners need to be expert communicators, presenting information effectively, capturing the spirit of the organisation (staying true to what it stands for) and at the same time motivating people to take action, either by giving money or helping to change society. Thankfully there are a number of tools to help.

*communication.*

## What tools can help?

In this book we cover a number of the promotional tools that you might be able to use to help with your work. They include:

## Printed material

Even the paper you use for letters gives out messages to the reader that might enhance or undermine the content of your campaign. We talk about design and production issues for various different types of printed material, and we also give some hints on writing effective corporate literature.

## Websites

Do not get a website just because everyone else has one. Websites can achieve a great deal for community groups if they have the right content and structure. We run through some of the key ingredients and highlight some of the fundraising options on the Internet. We also talk about how to keep your site fresh: in practical terms how to manage and maintain it, and creatively how to keep it lively and interesting.

## Video and audio

Video and audio can powerfully illustrate the important work of your organisation. Used well they are absorbing, make an emotional connection with their audience and demand further discussion or action. Each is a useful tool for fundraisers and campaigners. We run through the different ways you might use audio and video to promote your cause. In this section we describe the commissioning process and suggest ways of working in partnership with a production company to come up with a result that is most effective.

## The media

Despite the saying 'never believe what you read in the newspapers', people do tend to think that something is important once it has appeared in print, or been reported on radio or television. The media give you a way of reaching a wide audience in an instant, whether through editorial or advertising. We outline how to make use of both options and also describe the changing face of the media, with new opportunities opening up through digital broadcasting and very local radio and television.

## Open days, exhibitions, balls, conferences and roadshows

You will already know the value of meeting people face to face, and of being able to demonstrate in person just what it is that your organisation does. Live events – be they open days, exhibitions, balls, conferences or roadshows – give you the opportunity to meet people face to face in a fairly cost-effective way. They may even raise revenue for your organisation. In this section we run through some of the options available and then describe the processes involved in setting up such events.

## Presentations

Many outward-going, bubbly, confident people wilt when asked to stand up in front of a group of people to make a speech. But fundraisers and campaigners are called on to make all manner of presentations: talks at conferences, pitches to companies, speeches at fundraising events. Although there is no substitute for real-life practice, we run through some of the techniques that can help, and describe how to structure a presentation effectively.

## Merchandise

Branded products can help you get your organisation's name and identity into the public consciousness. If one of your donors is using your branded mousemat then they are less likely to forget you. If a potential donor has seen cars carrying stickers with a message about your organisation's work, they might be more receptive to a fundraising appeal. And if you come up with a striking design for mugs and T-shirts you might be able to sell them and raise some income too. We run through some of the essential things to remember if you want to build up a catalogue of merchandise, outlining different ways that you might make use of such products.

## Creative packages

You might want to make use of a number of different promotional elements in a package designed for members, school teachers or volunteer fundraisers, for instance. We explain how to approach the creation of such promotional packages.

## Finishing touches

There is always something more that you could do to get your organisation's message across: change the sign over the door, alter what is said on the answerphone, add information to all your e-mails. These and other 'finishing touches' are covered. They are suggestions to get you thinking about the 101 other things that could be done for your particular community group.

In each of the above sections we outline some of the most important considerations, explain how you might make use of the techniques, describe the key stages in the process, and suggest ways of budgeting. Before running through the areas in turn we look at the identity of your organisation or project and the audiences you deal with. After outlining the different promotional tools we provide further sources of information.

# 2

# Your identity

**Y**our organisation should have its own identity. When you go out to speak for your group you should not be promoting yourself. You should be promoting a set of values, ideas and activities that define a unique organisation. All of your promotional activity should be putting across a similar message about what is at the heart of your work.

Sometimes we need to take time out to reflect on just what it is that our work represents. What makes the organisation unique? What distinguishes a project from others? Unless you are clear about this it is not easy to promote your cause effectively. In this chapter we look at some of the issues of corporate identity (for your organisation or project).

**You will find some practical activities to help you:**

▶ define what makes your organisation special;
▶ find out what other people think of your organisation;
▶ brainstorm with colleagues about your organisation's unique qualities;
▶ identify your key audiences;
▶ develop a corporate identity.

## What is a corporate identity?

Corporate identity means more than having a recognisable logo. It is about having an agreed set of values and way of working that can then be reflected in the branding of your organisation or project. If you have a clear corporate identity then all of your promotional activities will reinforce each other. That hopefully means no wasted effort, no wasted resources, which has to be good for your organisation.

Consistency is absolutely vital for anyone promoting their organisation. Once you have agreed on what it is that your organisation stands for then this is what you need to get across. This is not an argument for spin doctors to keep you 'on message'. Instead it is about agreeing why your organisation exists and how different projects might help to advance this cause. It is important to spell this out so that people understand how they are contributing to the overall success of the organisation, whether as staff, volunteers, campaigners or fundraisers. If you are agreed about the things that are at the heart of your organisation, then you can come up with words, images and logos that help to convey this.

We are going to look at three essential stages in the development of a corporate or project identity:

1 **Defining your unique qualities:** What do you think distinguishes your project or organisation from others?
2 **Finding out what people think of you:** Who is it that you are trying to reach with your messages and how do they regard you?
3 **Creating corporate branding:** How do you reflect your unique qualities through branding that will appeal to your key audiences?

# Defining your unique qualities

Talking with colleagues is important in trying to identify what makes your organisation or project unique. Hopefully you will reach agreement on what the organisation stands for. If you can achieve this then you know that everyone is giving out consistent messages about your work. Your group's constitution will say what it is that your organisation was set up to achieve, but are you clear about how your organisation is different from others? What makes your group unique?

You may encounter some resistance from colleagues to the idea of discussing the organisation's identity. There is often a tension between those people who want to focus all time and resources on delivering your particular service and those wanting to raise awareness and funds. You may find it helpful to explain how your organisation's identity has clear links to service delivery. You need the input of project workers if you are to establish promotional materials that truly reflect the work of the organisation.

If people hear good things about your organisation and develop a sense of trust and loyalty then they will be more likely to use your services in future. Building a strong identity and positive reputation can attract clients to use your services. If your organisation is well known locally then you will also find it easier to attract additional volunteers and funders to support the group's work.

You do not have to sit through lengthy formal meetings with colleagues. There are a number of activities that you could take part in that are a lot of fun, but at the same time very revealing.

# Five activities to help you explore your organisation's unique qualities with colleagues

## Write a personal ad

How would you describe your organisation if you were placing an advert in a personal column? You know the sort of thing where 'young woman (gsoh) seeks fun-loving partner . . .' In this case it is the organisation that is doing the seeking and you are looking for a donor or supporter. How would you write such an ad in less than 30 words? It is a light-hearted activity but it can also be quite helpful in identifying what people think makes the group distinctive.

## Building on a reputation

Collect together some examples of leaflets or adverts that obviously build on a reputation for one service to introduce something else:

'You know X is a world-class gas supplier, but did you know we also offer cut-price electricity and low-cost phone calls?'

'For over 100 years X has been making traditional butter-baked biscuits, now we are launching an exciting new range of funky confectionery.'

The people writing these messages know what the general public think about their organisation and they have written their message accordingly. They assume some prior knowledge of an organisation. Show your examples to colleagues and ask them how they would write something similar for your organisation. Ask them to come up with some statements based on the formula: 'For over 20 years our charity has been known for X, now we're about to do Y.'

**The wordweb**

Write your organisation's name in a circle in the centre of a sheet of flipchart paper. Then write a word or phrase that comes into your mind when you think of the group. Add another, and so on linking relevant words with a line. Encourage colleagues to include value judgements as well as factual statements.

For example:

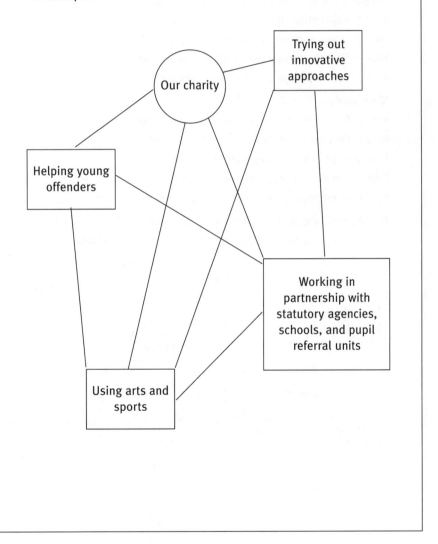

## The diamond of qualities

Write a series of words (values and qualities) that could be used to describe your organisation on a set of nine or 16 cards. Working as a group, place the cards in a diamond as follows:

**16 words**

Row 1: The most appropriate word (one word/phrase)
Row 2: Very appropriate (two words/phrases)
Row 3: Quite appropriate (three words/phrases)
Row 4: Appropriate (four words/phrases)
Row 5: Less appropriate (three words/phrases)
Row 6: Not very appropriate (two words/phrases)
Row 7: Least appropriate (one word/phrase)

**Nine words**

Row 1: The most appropriate word (one word/phrase)
Row 2: Very appropriate (two words/phrases)
Row 3: Appropriate (three words/phrases)
Row 4: Not very appropriate (two words/phrases)
Row 5: Least appropriate (one word/phrase)

This activity is good for generating discussion, particularly if you leave one card blank and then use it for an extra word/phrase.

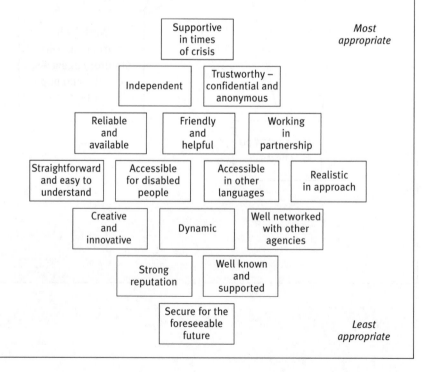

**Check out the competition**

Make a list of up to 10 organisations that might be considered 'competitors' because they might carry out similar work, be regarded as 'experts' on similar issues, or attract funding from similar sources. Beside each one list some of the ways in which you are different; use positive terms saying, 'We are different from X because we...' (do not knock the competition). By the time you have completed this activity you will have a list of really strong characteristics that make your organisation unique.

The activity could be done jointly with other agencies that share an interest in your particular area of work. You could work together to define how each organisation contributes something special to your campaigning.

## Reaching agreement

If everyone has been in clear agreement about the defining characteristics of your organisation then you can feed these details into the development of your corporate identity. You still need to find out the views of people outside the organisation and you also need to clarify who makes up your main audiences.

If, however, there is no consensus what should you do? The first thing to say is that this is not an unusual situation. Projects and organisations evolve over time, with people getting involved at different times and for different reasons. Community organisations are often working in areas where they are dealing directly with people's feelings, touching their lives. So, it is hardly surprising if you get a range of different reactions. People may have been affected differently by the organisation they work for.

But you do need to try to reach agreement, because if there is no common sense of purpose then messages to the outside world will be mixed and confusing. A good starting point may be your original trust deeds or, if your group is more informal, any original paperwork. Although organisations and projects change over time you should be able to see a strong connection with the founding objectives.

You may be able to resolve some of the differing opinions through discussion, but you might find it helpful to bring in an outside facilitator as someone independent to chair proceedings. However, sometimes it is not easy to just talk things through and reach agreement. You may want to draft a form of words that is circulated, so that people can add their comments and help shape things. It is also worth waiting for the results of any external research you carry out to see how you are perceived, and what others expect of you.

If opinion is still divided this may be an indication of deeper divisions in your organisation that go beyond the scope of this book. You may need someone to help mediate if you reach an impasse. Fortunately, many people will be more or less in agreement about the core values and unique qualities of their organisation. But what do people outside of your organisation think about you?

# Who are you trying to reach and what do they think of you?

Are you clear about whom you are trying to reach with your promotional messages? Unless you know whom you are talking to it is hard to know how you can create something that will appeal to them and be meaningful. This is probably the sort of question that requires some brainstorming with colleagues under the following headings.

## Main target audience

Your main target audience includes the people that you want to reach most of the time with your promotional messages: promoting your cause, promoting a project or promoting an appeal. These are the people that should be given greatest consideration when coming up with your corporate identity. They are the people whom you want to communicate with on a regular basis, who need to see instantly that a letter or promotional item is from your group, and who probably already have an opinion about what your organisation stands for.

Under this heading you may want to list the main groups of people who use your services, your main beneficiaries. You may also want to include the most important funders or supporters of your organisation.

A welfare organisation providing transport and lunch facilities for older people wanted to revamp its corporate identity. The charity had a young graphic designer among its group of volunteers and asked her to come up with a new logo. When she produced a design the trustees felt immediately that it was not right. On reflection they realised that while the design used an image that was appropriate – symbolising outreach and care – the colours were garish and clashing and would not appeal to their main audiences. Both beneficiaries and key funders were drawn from an older and more traditional group of people.

## Secondary audiences

There will be other people you want to reach too with your literature and other promotional activities. You want them to know about your organisation and your work, but they will not be your main consideration in designing your corporate identity.

Under this heading you may want to include some types of funders who are less regular supporters: key opinion-formers; other community organisations; and the general public, for instance.

## What do people think about your organisation?

If your project or organisation has been in existence for some time then it has some sort of history, a reputation. What has your organisation come to mean to people? What does it stand for? You need to know before you start to think about all the new messages you have to give people. You might have to correct a few misconceptions, you might have to convert people to a whole new way of thinking, or you might be able to build on an extraordinarily positive reputation.

If you are just beginning a new project or creating a new organisation then you still need to find out what people think about your area of work, how well they think other organisations have approached the issues and what they think is needed.

So how do you find out what people think about your organisation or the area of work in which you are involved?

# Market research

A large charity might consider commissioning market research to find out people's opinions about the organisation. The researchers would work with a sample of several hundred or thousand people, and may then complement this with in-depth research with a small group of people. The first part of the research (surveying hundreds of people) would come up with some interesting statistics highlighting people's immediate reactions to questions about your organisation. The focus group work would elaborate with explanations about why people feel a certain way about your organisation, giving more depth to the earlier responses.

You might not be able to afford to engage an independent market research company, but you can still carry out an informative survey yourself. If you do so then there are certain things to bear in mind.

### Consider different ways to carry out your research

There are different approaches that you can use to gather information of this kind:

- **Informal:** You might simply sit down with a group of relevant people and chat about certain areas of your work, under pre-agreed headings.
- **Formal questionnaires:** Alternatively you might draw up a questionnaire which can be distributed in various ways. These can be posted out, with a reply-paid envelope; faxed or posted out with a fax-back sheet to encourage quick responses; e-mailed; or run through face-to-face with the respondent.

### Be clear about whom you are surveying

Think about your main target audiences before embarking on any survey. If you rely heavily on public donations for your work, then you will want to know what the general public thinks about your organisation. However, if your main sources of income are trusts and local authorities and your beneficiaries are clearly defined, you may want to speak to these people specifically.

### Consider face-to-face survey work

Although asking the questions in person is more labour intensive than sending out questionnaires it means you are on hand to answer any queries. It also ensures you get a response.

- **Introduce yourself:** Explain who you are clearly at the outset of any interview, and provide written evidence. Ask politely if the person you have approached is able to spare five or ten minutes (depending on the length of the survey). State the name of your organisation and a little about what you do without influencing the results of the research. Also outline the importance of the survey to the future development of your group. Any survey of this kind should be conducted in a professional way that will enhance the organisation's reputation.

- **Focus groups:** In small groups ask open questions; these are questions that will prompt more than a 'yes' or 'no' response. You start open questions with 'How', 'Why', 'Who', 'What', 'Where' and 'When' rather than 'Do you'. Be clear about how you are going to record the proceedings. Will you use video or audio-tape or a notetaker?

An environmental charity invited a group of individual donors who had supported them over a number of years to take part in a small focus group. They provided the organisation with valuable information about why they continued to give money and what they found special about the charity.

This provided the fundraiser with information about the particular characteristics of the charity that prompted donors to give (and may prompt others to do so). Importantly, it also demonstrated to those donors just how much they were valued. When the fundraiser asked for ideas on how to reach other potential donors, two of those in the group volunteered to become actively involved in recruiting new supporters.

## What do you do with this information?

It is all very well collecting information about how you and others see the organisation, but what can you do as a result? If the results highlight lots of goodwill among the general public for your work, then you can build on the things they say they particularly like. You can draw attention to them in literature and publicity.

An industrial therapy organisation working with young adults with learning disabilities carried out a survey amongst people who employed the organisation to carry out work for them. Before conducting the research the project coordinator had assumed that the majority of clients (local businesses) were interested in being given a professional service, on time, in budget and at the same time making a positive contribution to the local community. What became clear from the survey was that whilst all these things were important, many clients were greatly interested in the people working there. They wanted to know more about the staff, and wanted them to be more 'visible'.

As a result the charity held more open days and introduced a newsletter with information about the staff. The annual report was transformed to include case study reports on many of the staff. All of these changes received warm feedback from clients, who said that it increased the likelihood of their using the service in future.

If the results show there is a gap between your view of the organisation and the view of the general public, then you know that you need to build people's awareness of your work.

An organisation working with young people at risk of crime offers a range of diversionary activities including sport, creative work and a cyber cafe. When they ran a survey amongst local people they found they were viewed as the 'drugs project'. People felt that the group was doing positive work in this area, but associated them with combating drug misuse. The organisation knew that it had to raise awareness of its other activities to show the breadth and depth of its work. One thing they did was to introduce a slogan that ran on all of its materials including banners and public signs saying 'Offering young people art, sport and computer skills to help change their lives'.

## Creating corporate branding

Once you are clear about all those things that make your organisation or project unique, who you are trying to reach and what they think of you, then you are in a position to come up with appropriate branding. This might be to bring your organisation up to date, or perhaps to create an identity for a new initiative.

Three of the key ingredients are:

- a name
- a logo
- a 'look and feel'.

# The right name

Unless you are going to employ an expensive team of consultants, the best way to come up with the right name – for an organisation or for a particular project or campaign – is to brainstorm with colleagues, service users, volunteers and others likely to be affected by your work. In recent years some big companies have gone for names that join together bits of words to form a new word. The result can sound mildly exotic yet not be very enlightening about the nature of the company's work.

Charities have tended to stick to names that quickly indicate something about that organisation and its work. Even if you have never had anything to do with Crime Concern or Age Concern you would have a pretty good idea what they do from their names. This makes a lot of sense when there are so many different audiences to reach out to. Service users, for instance, look for help and support when they reach crisis point. They do not research available help beforehand. They will reach for a directory and see a name; if it looks relevant then they might ring. If you had been the victim of a crime and needed support, you would know intuitively that the right place to seek help was from Victim Support.

Policy-makers are lobbied each day by numerous individuals and organisations. If your name is clear and to the point then they will instantly know that your opinion is going to be relevant to their work. Funding organisations receive hundreds of applications from voluntary and community groups. They want to fund organisations that work in particular ways to help specific groups of people. Your name may show them that there is a match between their aims and your area of work. Of course there is still much more to be done before you can persuade them to invest in your project, but it is a start. Individual members of the public are also bombarded with literature. Again, knowing the type of organisation that is contacting them can mean the difference between a leaflet being read and thrown straight into the bin.

These are arguments for using a straightforward name, perhaps along with a strapline as part of your logo (see below).

## Logos

A logo is an organisation's distinctive badge. It can be a mixture of the following elements:

- the organisation's name in a special font (and colour);
- symbols, patterns or icons;
- an image;
- a strapline (quick message).

A new voluntary organisation successfully attracted major lottery funding, local government support and money from central government. After months of negotiation and lobbying the group suddenly had to be up and running. To save time and money a member of the small staff team quickly came up with a logo to 'tide them over'. Soon the organisation needed a brochure to help explain its work, it needed a letterhead, it needed a website. All carried the logo, which was just intended to fill an immediate gap. Several months down the line, the organisation wanted to invest in a corporate identity, but felt that funders would be unhappy if all the brochures, literature and website carrying the initial logo had to be replaced.

A logo needs to be simple, memorable and easy to reproduce in a whole variety of formats. Here are a couple of things to bear in mind if you are using colours in your logo.

Come up with an alternative black and white and single-colour version (so that you will be able to keep the cost of printing manageable and so that you have options available if your logo is being used on other people's materials).

Use colours that are easy to reproduce through the four colour printing process (*see p39 for further information*). If you come up with a logo with a number of very vibrant distinctive colours then each time you print something you will have to use extra inks to reproduce the precise colour (and this can be expensive).

Other practical questions to ask yourself when designing or reviewing a logo are:

- Will it work on a very large or very small scale?
- Will it fax and photocopy acceptably?

More design-focused questions to consider include:

- Is there an obvious connection between the logo and the work we do?

- Does the logo suggest colours or a style that we can repeat in our literature so that people get a feel for our material?
- If the logo is replacing an existing one, will people we work with see a subtle link between the two?

When the logo is first agreed and launched you will have a pretty good idea about how it should be used. But other people will not know this information unless you come up with some guidelines. Larger organisations have strict style guides that outline how the logo can be used in a wide variety of situations. In the case of smaller community groups it is probably more appropriate to give guidance on how the logo is to be reproduced:

- in colour (four colours or more, with colour reference numbers if appropriate);
- in one or two colours;
- in black and white;
- reversed out (like a negative, white where black would be and vice versa).

Here is an example.

Although Awards for All is a funder rather than a charity, the logo is a good example of a memorable 'badge' and a name that says what it is all about – with a strapline to provide even more clarification.

## Developing a 'look and feel'

Having an appropriate name and logo does not guarantee consistency in your promotional work and the instant recognisability that you are looking for. This recognisability factor only comes when there is something distinctive about your promotional materials that instantly says this is from your organisation. Often such a look and feel evolves over time. You create something that people really like and then you repeat the successful elements in the next thing you do. This sounds a bit hit and miss, however, and an expensive way of developing an identity.

You could decide at the outset that you not only want to agree a name and logo, but that you also want to agree the whole look and feel. Some of the things that contribute to a look and feel are:

- **Colours:** You might agree that all materials are based around the colours in your logo or a few additional agreed colours.
- **Typeface:** You might agree on a font that you will use in all printed materials, including letters, as well as promotional items.
- **Imagery:** You might agree on a certain approach to images in your promotional materials. Perhaps you will always use illustrations by a particular artist, or maybe you will always use close up photos by a particular photographer.
- **Document formats:** You might come up with some sample layouts that form the basis of a range of printed materials, your website, powerpoint presentations, and so on.

All of this information, along with samples and instructions on how to use the logo, can be put together in a folder or style guide so that there is an easy reference manual for others to consult.

## Ensuring everyone has access

There will be people you want to reach who might miss out on your message if you do not ensure it is accessible, perhaps because of a disability or because English is not their first language. This might mean offering materials in other languages, providing literature on tape or in Braille and using a sign language interpreter in presentations or on videos.

Your local council will have details of a community interpreting and translation service. The community interpreting service can advise you on the common community languages used in a particular area and they offer a variety of translation services. The RNIB and Talking Newspaper Association can advise on how to make materials accessible to blind and partially sighted people by using large print, Braille and audio tapes.

If you need to work with a sign language interpreter then you can find details of services through the CACDP (Council for the Advancement of Communication with Deaf People). The website www.cacdp.demon.co.uk has information about interpreters, speech to text translators, lipspeakers and deafblind interpreters.

Other people with disabilities in your audience may have special communication access requirements that you have not anticipated. To ensure they know that you will make every effort to give them access, you might include a statement or invite people to make contact for information in other formats. The Disability Rights Commission provides a valuable list of links to websites of specialist disability organisations. The important thing is to find out from your audience how you could make your communication more accessible. Invite feedback and act on it.

There is a cost involved in making materials accessible, and you will need a line in your budget to cover this expenditure. This is an investment in reaching potential donors and clients who are disabled or who use other community languages.

You will find useful contact details at the end of the book under *Further information* on p110.

# 3

# Printed material

This chapter focuses on printed material. First we talk generally about writing promotional material. Then we look at design issues. We examine different types of printed material and run through the main stages in the print production process.

**This chapter will help you to:**

▶ write and design effective printed material;
▶ develop a corporate identity and literature;
▶ create materials in different print formats;
▶ understand the print production process and cost options.

## The importance of printed materials

The much talked about paper-less office never materialised. The Internet has opened up many new opportunities, but we seem to have just as many brochures, leaflets, posters, postcards, newsletters and other printed material arrive each day.

Printed material remains an essential communication tool for fundraisers and campaigners. In many cases it might be the only medium you use to make contact with hundreds, perhaps thousands, of people: explaining your work, asking for money and inviting them to take action. It is therefore essential that community organisations use print effectively. That means writing punchy persuasive copy, using design creatively, and adopting a style or brand identity that is appropriate and used consistently.

## Writing effectively

When you are writing a piece of campaign or fundraising literature you want people to respond in certain ways:

- **emotionally** – engaging people so that they care about your cause and become committed to the purpose of your work;

- **logically** – persuading people with your arguments so they see the sense of what you are saying and how you are addressing the issues;
- **actively** – showing people how they can support your work and prompting them to do so.

It is impossible to give a formula that will work in all cases, but there are some techniques you can use to help.

## Engaging people emotionally

Use case histories, particularly examples written in the first person. A personal testimony can be used to make a point very powerfully. Use illustrations (pictures, poems, creative writing) by service users in the literature. People connect with other people not statistics. Explain how people will benefit if the reader becomes involved.

## Persuading people logically

Bring arguments to life with tangible examples: if you were to do X then we could do Y; if we did Y then this would mean Z. What would happen if your service did not exist? How would people be worse off? How will they be better off with your support?

## Prompting action

Include examples of what other people have done to support your work. Make it easy to take action: include a reply slip, freephone number, e-mail address, form to fax back.

# Techniques to consider

Here are some techniques to consider when writing promotional literature.

## Keep your audience in mind

If you are developing something that has to be relevant to a wide audience then you need to:

- take care not to assume too much knowledge, but at the same time not to patronise. If in doubt, invite someone independent to review your material and let you know if it could be made clearer or more appropriate;
- avoid jargon (whether specialist to your organisation or to the community sector). Not everyone is familiar with the latest buzzwords. Depending on the type of document you may need to include a glossary;

- give fair weight to any mention of funders (they could be part of the audience);
- include sources of further information.

If you are creating something for a specialist audience, such as health professionals or local authority officers, then you need to:

- give them credit for their area of expertise, but at the same time explain those things that will be less familiar to them;
- give specific examples that help them to identify with your work;
- invite one of these specialists to review your material and let you know of any adjustments that could help.

## Keep information in bite-sized pieces

Use short words and short sentences. Use sub-headings to break up text and signpost different bits of information.

## Keep it clear

Be clear about the purpose of the literature and state this at the beginning of the material. This helps the reader to know what to expect. It also helps you to stay focused.

## Keep it simple

Write as you speak, unless you are producing a document that has to be a formal committee paper, for instance. People who are more used to writing 'business-speak' can find it hard to loosen up; they talk about 'purchasing' something instead of 'buying' it, for instance. When you have written something ask yourself, 'Is this something that I'd say if I was chatting to friends or colleagues?' If it is not then perhaps you should simplify your language.

Compare the following texts:

> After due consideration the committee has prioritised the establishment of joined-up working with the local authority social services department in our bid to build the capacity of disadvantaged families with challenging children during times of distress.

> We want to help families who are finding it difficult to bring up their children, by working with local social workers.

## Keep it real

Incorporate real-life examples, in people's own words where possible.

**Keep checking**

Re-read what you have written to see if it flows. Invite a third party to read the material too: to check for spelling mistakes, but more importantly to ensure it makes sense to them.

**Ensure design is appropriate**

Help people by using the design of your printed materials to support the content. Do not let clever design get in the way of your message.

# Using design creatively

Most voluntary organisations now have access to a computer. This means that it is possible to lay out text so that it looks quite attractive. If you want something a bit more creative with a look and feel that get a reaction then you might need to commission a graphic designer.

# Designing something yourself

Desktop publishing packages mean that we can all produce leaflets and basic newsletters that incorporate pictures and different fonts. The following points will help you to create designs that are simple and effective.

- Stick to one or two fonts for most of your text to help it look clean and easy to read.
- Use fonts that are sans-serif (that is they do not have curls or flourishes on the j's, f's, g's, y's, etc.) if you want to keep the look simple. This bullet point has been set in a sans-serif font as an example.
- A reader's eye moves across the page from top left downwards and designs should generally reflect this. Do not completely break the middle of a column of text with a picture. The reader's eye will naturally move to the top of the next column and they might miss out some vital information.
- Incorporate 'white space' so that the page can 'breathe'. Text packed too tightly is off-putting.
- Come up with an overall theme or grid and use it throughout (*see examples on p28*). You can make exceptions, but only for emphasis.
- Consider your audience; look at other printed material aimed at similar groups of people and echo the bits you like.

# DSC Newsletter

## A critical time for the voluntary sector according to new report

Re-read what you have written to see if it flows. Invite a third party to read the material too to check for spelling mistakes, but more importantly to ensure it makes sense to them. Re-read what you have written to see if it flows. Invite a third party to read the material too to check for spelling mistakes, but more importantly to ensure it makes sense to them. Re-read what you have written to see if it flows. Invite a third party to read the material too to check for spelling mistakes, but more importantly to ensure it makes sense to them. Re-read what you have written to see if it flows, but more importantly to ensure it makes sense to them. Re-read what you have written to see if it flows. Invite a third party to read the material too to check for spelling mistakes, but more importantly to ensure it makes sense to them. Re-read what you have written to see if it flows. Invite a third party to read the material too to check for spelling mistakes, but more importantly to ensure it makes sense to them.

Re-read what you have written to see if it flows. Invite a third party to read the material too to check for spelling mistakes, but more importantly to ensure it makes sense to them. Re-read what you have written to see if it flows. Invite a third party to read the material too to check for spelling mistakes, but more importantly to ensure it makes sense to them. Re-read what you have written to see if it flows. Invite a third party to read the material too to check for spelling mistakes, but more importantly to ensure it makes sense to them. Re-read what you have written to see if it flows. Invite a third party to read the material too to check for spelling mistakes, but more importantly to ensure it makes sense to them.

### Adventurous design

Re-read what you have written to see if it flows. Invite a third party to read the material too to check for spelling mistakes, but more importantly to ensure it makes sense to them. Re-read what you have written to see if it flows, but more importantly to ensure it makes sense to them. Re-read what you have written to see if it flows. Invite a third party to read the material too to check for spelling mistakes, but more importantly to ensure it makes sense to them. Re-read what you have written to see if it flows. Invite a third party to read the material too to check for spelling mistakes, but more importantly to ensure it makes sense to them. Re-read what you have written to

But more importantly to ensure it makes sense to them. Re-read what you have written to see if it flows. Invite a third party to read the material too to check for spelling mistakes, but more importantly to ensure it makes sense to them. Re-read what you have written to see if it flows. Invite a third party to read the material too to check for spelling mistakes, but more importantly to ensure it makes sense to them. Re-read what you have written to see if it flows. Invite a third party to read the material

ensure it makes sense to them. Re-read what you have written to see if it flows. Invite a third party to read the material too to check for spelling mistakes, but more importantly to ensure it makes

*An example of a two-column grid.*

---

# DSC Fortnightly

## Charities face a shot across their bows as government inquiry is published

makes sense to them. Re-read what you have written to see if it flows. Invite a third party to read the material too to check for spelling mistakes, but more importantly to ensure it makes sense to them. Re-read what you have written to see if it flows, but more importantly to ensure it makes sense to them. Re-read what you have written to see if it flows. Invite a third party to read the material too to check for spelling mistakes, but more importantly to ensure it makes sense to them. Re-read what you have written to see if it flows, but more importantly to ensure it makes sense to them. Re-read what you have written to see if it flows. Invite a third party to read the material too to check for spelling mistakes, but more importantly to ensure it makes sense to them. Re-read what you have written to see if it flows, but more importantly to ensure it makes sense to them. Re-read what you have written to see if it flows. Invite a third party to read the material too to check for spelling mistakes, but more importantly to ensure it makes sense to them. Re-read what you have written to

s, but more importantly to ensure it makes sense to them. Re-read what you have written to see if it flows. Invite a third party to read the material too to check for spelling mistakes, but more importantly to ensure it makes sense to them. Re-read what you have written to see if it flows. Invite a third party to read the material

### Adventurous design projects

makes sense to them. Re-read what you have written to see if it flows. Invite a third party to read the material too to check for spelling mistakes, but more importantly to ensure it makes sense to them. Re-read what you have written to see if it flows. But more importantly to ensure it makes sense to them. Re-read what you have written to see if it flows. Invite a third party to read the material too to check for spelling mistakes, but more importantly to ensure it makes sense to them. Re-read what you have written to see if it flows. Invite a third party to read the material too to check for spelling mistakes, but more importantly to ensure it makes sense to them. Re-read what you have written to

importantly to ensure it makes sense to them. Re-read what you have written to s, but more importantly to ensure it makes sense to them. Re-read what you have written to see if it flows. Invite a third party to read the material too to check for spelling

mistakes, but more importantly to ensure it makes sense to them. Re-read what you have written to see if it flows. Invite a third party to read the material too to check for spelling mistakes, but more importantly to ensure it makes sense to them. Re-read what you have written to see if it flows. Re-read what you then. Re-read what you then. Re-read what you then. Re-read what you then. Re-read what you then. Re-read what you then. Re-read what you have written to s, but more importantly to ensure it makes sense to them. Re-read what you have written to see if it flows. Invite a third party to read the material too to check for spelling mistakes, but more importantly to ensure it makes sense to them. Re-read what you have written to see if it flows. Invite a third party to read the material too to check for spelling mistakes, but more importantly to ensure it makes sense to them. Re-read what you have

### NOTICE

makes sense to them. Re-read what you have written to see if it flows. Invite a third party to read the material too to check for spelling mistakes, but more importantly to ensure it makes sense to them. Re-read what you have written to see if it flows. Invite a third party to read the material too to check for spelling mistakes, but more importantly to ensure it makes sense to them. Re-read what you have written to see if it flows, but more importantly to ensure it makes sense to them. Re-read what you have written to see if it flows. Invite a third party to read the material too to check for spelling mistakes, but more f

*An example of a three-column grid.*

# Using a design company

If you want a more adventurous design then you need to work with someone who can provide professional artistic input. You might employ someone within the organisation, but if not you will need to think about commissioning a design company. Below we give some guidance if you are thinking of doing so.

1   Come up with a clear brief with the following information:

- **about your organisation** – what you stand for, your main areas of work, and any corporate identity issues;
- **about the project** – its aims and objectives, who will benefit, key words or phrases to describe the work;
- **about the literature** – who it is for, how it relates to other materials, any ideas on format (size, page numbers, etc.), what you want it to achieve;
- **suggested approaches** – ideas on what you like and do not like to steer them a little. You might also indicate the available budget.

2   Send the brief to up to three design companies. You could simply look in your Yellow Pages for local graphic designers. However, it is advisable to ask for recommendations from other voluntary organisations. If you have seen something that you particularly like, then ask who designed it. You are much more likely to find a company you can work with if you like some of the work they have already produced, if they have an understanding of the sector, and if they have a good reputation with other community groups.

3   Invite them to submit examples of their work and ideas for this particular project. State that there is no fee payable for this initial tendering stage.

4   Ask for prices that you can compare: for a daily rate, the design costs involved in developing a concept for the literature, and possibly a per page design cost. Also invite them to provide you with their terms and conditions, which often include additional charges for corrections and scanning pictures.

Taking into account the designers' approach, price and ideas, you can make a decision about who to work with. You might want to work with them on something quite small to begin with. This gives you a chance to see if you like working with them and also whether you like their style. Better to iron out problems with a small piece of work than to embark on a corporate redesign and discover a clash of personalities and ideas.

# Corporate letterhead

If you have a logo you might feel that you are well on the way to having your letterhead completed. This is not always the case.

> A church-based social support organisation commissioned a new logo and letterhead. The team quickly agreed on the most appropriate logo. It captured the caring and spiritual side to the organisation, while building effectively on a previous logo, but giving it a more modern feel. However, when it came to the letterhead the team was split. Some wanted individually personalised letterheads. Others thought this extravagant and preferred a single letterhead for the whole team. There was still more disagreement over where the address and telephone details should appear on the page, with some preferring a block of text in the top right hand corner, and others wanting the information scrolled across the bottom.

These, then, are some of the points to consider when deciding on letterhead design:

- You need to include legally required information such as your charity number and VAT number.
- You must decide where the main contact details should appear. This might mean a line across the page (top or bottom), a block of text (in either margin) or even text on the reverse of the main sheet (although this increases the print costs).
- Consider how easy it is to set up a letter layout on the page; it is amazing how many logos intrude over the right hand margin of the page.

> An organisation supporting unemployed adults thanks its supporters by adding a message onto its letterhead each year: 'Thanks to the £100,000 kindly donated in 1998, 300 people are now in employment, 150 have received training and 70 have gone into fulltime education.'

# Using postcards, bookmarks, posters and flyers

There are many different types of printed material that you can use to promote your cause. We are going to look at some of the different smaller scale printed materials that can have a high impact for fundraisers and campaigners. They can be used to get your message out to a large number of people at a relatively low cost. They might be the way you get in touch with many of these people for the first time.

## Postcards

Postcards can be a powerful campaigning tool when they combine arresting images with strong direct messages. You can send them out yourself, or you can make them available for others to buy or pick up and send on to others. The postcards can be created specifically to promote a particular message, or they can demonstrate the results of a project.

A digital art project with young people focusing on bullying created a series of postcards. In developing the postcards the young people discussed their own experiences and came up with strategies to deal with bullying in different settings. The process of producing the postcards helped educate the participants, and the postcards were used with other young people to get messages across about bullying. The organisation leading the work has also used them to:

- share ideas about bullying with policy and decision makers locally;
- promote its work more generally to funders, showing the high quality outcome.

Before you create a postcard for your organisation it is worth gathering together some samples of other people's efforts. You will find postcards in cinema lobbies, at some pub entrances, as well as in shops and tourist attractions. You will quickly discover what you like and dislike in a postcard, and you will also see some of the essential information to include on the reverse. Do not forget to leave space for the user to add their own message.

If you are thinking about creating a series of postcards then talk to your printer about how to save money by positioning several postcards over the space of an A4 sheet of card which is later cut down to size.

# Bookmarks

Like postcards bookmarks have a use beyond that of just giving information. They too can carry simple direct messages, and they are a fairly low-cost way of spreading your message.

You can encourage a response to a message on a postcard if you invite people to send it somewhere or to someone. You obviously cannot do this with a bookmark. So how can you make the bookmark more interactive, so that it is not just carrying a slogan? You might signpost people to a website; the link here is that you are inviting them to put an electronic bookmark at that site.

A conservation charity ran a campaign with its local libraries, using bookmarks. Every borrower over a month-long initiative was given the charity's bookmark. The bookmark's message was 'I'm here to help you so that you can help the environment . . . I'll remind you of where you've got to with your book if you stop reading for a while to take part in our Millennium clean up . . .'

# Flyers

Flyers range from glossy slick documents to simple black and white photocopies. They can give out quite a lot of information and prompt responses by including reply slips and telephone response numbers. Flyers come in many shapes and sizes. The more unusual the shape and size, generally, the more expensive they are to design and print: the paper has to be cut to a custom size and shape.

Small A5 sheets (half the size of normal letterhead) are a good size because they mean you have to use short sharp messages to fit your text into the available space. You have to keep it simple and direct. A strong image, key information and instructions for how to respond are all that is needed.

A4 (the size of normal letterhead) gives you room to use more pictures, perhaps a case study to demonstrate the effect of your work and give quite a bit of information. They are not as handy to hold and distribute, but they are the sort of size used for posters in community buildings and so might be pinned up on a noticeboard.

Your flyer will be competing with many others in someone's in-tray or shopping bag. How do you ensure they read yours? Here are some things to increase the impact of a flyer:

- Use a large simple heading that invites the reader to find out more, perhaps by asking a question.
- Ensure about a fifth of the page is blank ('white space') so that the text does not feel crammed.
- Use an image that intrigues and invites more questions.
- Use a quote either as a heading or as a large piece of text.

## Posters

A good poster often has a strong image to attract attention, but sometimes it is a well-phrased question or remark. Most space is given over to the eye-catching element, with some room for explanation. Occasionally there will not be an explanation, when the poster is part of a series of materials and is meant to tease us a little. For most community groups, though, the thought of a piece of promotional material teasing people rather than putting over a message seems like a luxury. It usually makes more sense for everything to be self-contained so that every item is working for us.

Posters can be run off on desktop colour printers or they can be produced through a print company. If you want them to last then you might consider getting them laminated, particularly if they are going to be displayed outdoors. A printer can arrange lamination for you.

## Creating folders and booklets

Folders and booklets provide further fairly detailed information. They will usually have been requested by someone who wants to know more about your campaign. Occasionally you may use them when approaching someone 'cold', but they are not usually used in a direct marketing campaign. This affects the way you write the contents. Where postcards and flyers are quite pushy – quickly making their point and asking for something in return – these larger documents can be more subtle.

A good practice guide to supporting looked-after children was written to show professionals how they could work together and to show policy-makers why they should invest in this cooperative approach. The whole brochure followed one individual's story. The account was gripping from the first page and the case was made very effectively.

Folders give you flexibility to mix and match the contents, and they are quite a cost-effective approach. They can be used in a variety of contexts: to promote your cause at conferences; to send out further information material in response to requests; and to present supporting materials in funding applications, for instance. Ask your printer or designer for samples. Some are pre-cut so they cost less than custom-made folders.

Folders work well when you are presenting discrete chunks of information that can naturally be divided up onto different sheets. So, if you offer a range of different services, for instance, these could be presented on individual sheets. If you are trying to get a number of projects off the ground, again these could be outlined on different inserts. If you are telling more of a story – an annual report, an overview of the organisation – then a booklet is more appropriate.

In both the case of the folder and the booklet it is important to signpost the contents and also to state clearly the purpose of the literature.

# Producing newsletters

Newsletters are a great way of promoting your cause to people who are already in touch with your organisation. On the face of it a newsletter is there to share news about progress and projects, but there are a number of ways of slipping in messages about specific campaigns and funding opportunities. A report on a successful sponsored project could simply include a positive quote from the sponsoring organisation. You might go a stage further and include a small box beside the article outlining similar sponsorship opportunities. Campaigners can be more direct in newsletters than fundraisers. It would feel perfectly OK to have articles about the launch of a new campaign, the results of a campaign and requests for volunteers to take on a more active role in future campaigns.

Here are some tips to help you produce effective newsletters:

- Draw up a timetable for the next 12 months with deadlines for the supply of articles, editing, design and printing/photocopying, and distribution. Stick to it!
- Do not be over ambitious. If you are struggling with resources either reduce the number of times you bring out a newsletter in a year or reduce the size of it.
- Mimic newspapers in your layout: have a grid with columns. Run some articles down a single column, and run others across a couple of columns.
- Give your newsletter issue numbers and store back copies.
- Make your newsletter interactive by inviting feedback and comments.

- Do not be afraid of making editorial comments that express a point of view. You do not have to be neutral.
- Include articles by a range of different people so that you get a mixture of styles of writing.
- Only use good quality pictures. Better to use no picture than to use a fuzzy photograph.
- Find out if people would prefer to receive e-newsletters. If you embed the newsletter in the e-mail itself then there is no design involved, you cut down on production and distribution costs, and it takes less time to produce.

For more on newsletters, see *The DIY Guide to Charity Newsletters*, which is listed under *Further information* on p110.

# Producing an annual report

Your annual report is not just a source of information; it is also an important promotional item. It is a place where you can record all the achievements of the past year, document your thanks to workers and supporters and set out your plans for the future (which need additional support to succeed).

The tone of the report should be positive, upbeat and fairly chatty. This is a document with a wide circulation to a general audience. The content should be a mixture of information about the organisation's progress, individual projects, specific case studies and plans for the future.

Keep the information brief and to the point. A project description should be perhaps two or three paragraphs. A good annual report will give a flavour of the work; photographs will capture important moments and moods. The legally required information will be there. The reader should get a sense of the purpose of the organisation, a feeling of progress.

Large corporations have to impress investors with flashy reports. Charities and community organisations also have investors, but there is a danger that an over-glossy annual report may put people off. It could give the impression the organisation has too much money sloshing around. The answer may be to produce a nice-looking colourful document with a limited number of pages (up to around eight pages, say). Such annual reports look professional but they do not feel like a waste of money.

If you outline your future plans, then your annual report becomes the launch-pad for forthcoming appeals and helps put such appeals in context. It also means that when you contact people in the future they will have a vague recollection of what you are talking about, so they are more likely to be receptive when you ask for support.

For more information on this topic, see *How to Produce Inspiring Annual Reports* (details under *Further information* on p110).

# Main stages in the print production process

Sometimes lovely looking leaflet designs go off to the printer and come back looking almost as lovely yet completely different. The colour of document you see on a computer screen is different from the colour you get from printing with four inks.

It is helpful to know some of the main stages in the print production process if you want to avoid disappointing results.

1 **Design and layout:** Check with the printers that the programme you are using for design is compatible with their computers if you are doing the work yourself. If you are working with a designer then make sure you make all corrections before the material goes to print. Whilst it is still on the designer's computer you have the opportunity to make lots of tweaks. Some designers charge for every correction, others make a charge for each version they produce. As soon as your artwork goes to the printer's then every single change costs money.

2 **Pre-press:** The printer will prepare the artwork (i.e. your piece of literature), firstly ensuring that no glitches have occurred in moving a computer file from one machine to another. It is amazing how often simply opening a file on another computer throws out an alignment so it is worth asking for a proof to check against. Then if your literature is being printed on a litho press the printer will produce a screen or film for each page. If you pay extra you can have a further proof copy at this stage. If your literature is being printed digitally then no film is produced; the printing is done straight from the computer.

3 **Printing:** Your literature might be printed in one, two, four or more colours depending on your design and how much you pay. Check with the printer about how long the printing will take and build this into your schedule.

4 **Finishing:** Once the printing is complete there is further work to be done, such as applying a gloss or matt finish, drying, stapling or binding, collation. Give strict instructions so that you can be sure that the whole job is going to be completed to your satisfaction.

5 **Delivery:** Finally, ensure you have arrangements in place for delivery and storage.

# Distribution

How do you get your materials out to the right people? If you have a limited number of very active supporters then this might not be much of a problem. You could have a committee of 10 people who are in regular contact with everyone you want to reach. Just hand them a batch of literature and off they go. But if you want to distribute your material more widely how can you do this effectively? You may or may not know where you want the material to end up.

## If you have names and addresses

You may have a mailing list, or you may be running a campaign where people get in touch to request copies of literature. In either case you have the contact details for the final destination of your materials. You simply need to sort out the mechanics for getting the literature there.

There are a number of mailing companies or 'houses' that might help you. They will store the documents and then 'fulfil' orders (i.e. produce an address label, put the relevant material in an envelope and mail out). Such organisations are listed in Yellow Pages. Another option is to do it yourself, but storage can sometimes be a major problem, along with the volume of work involved. There are also industrial therapy organisations in most major towns or cities that provide fulfilment services. Your local CVS will probably have details.

## If you do not have names and addresses

If you want to make materials available to a wide audience and do not have names and addresses, then you could ask coordinators or managers of the following public places to take some of your materials:

- local library
- local supermarket
- village hall or community building
- civic centre/local authority building
- leisure centre
- cinema
- shopping centre.

This approach helps you to reach new people. It also means that you can post out a number of documents at a time to one location, cutting down on the distribution and fulfilment costs. But it is less targeted, and if you want to reach a certain audience this method may not be appropriate.

# Setting a budget

There are two main ways in which you will probably budget a piece of print. One is to have an idea of what you want to achieve: you can invite printers to tell you how much this will cost. The other way is to have a limited budget for a job: you need to invite printers to quote on various options.

Below we set out the main items to include in your budget.

### Writing

This should either cover the cost of your time or of commissioning someone.

### Photography

If you take your own pictures there will still be the cost of materials to account for.

### Illustrations

You might commission an illustrator or use work produced by service users (who should be paid a fee).

### Design and layout

This might be part of your brief to a printer if they offer this service. Design costs can divide up into the initial design concept and then the layout of each page, plus scans and proof copies.

### Print costs

These will probably include proof costs, possibly scans, print production, possibly lamination, and delivery.

### Distribution

This will depend on whether you are mailing literature or hand delivering.

**A printer's brief would include:**

**The format:** This covers the size and shape and number of pages. A4 is the standard size of a letter; A5 is half this size; A3 is twice the size of A4.

**The print run:** This is the number of copies with a quote for 'run ons'. (Run on costs show how much it would cost to produce additional documents whilst this lot are being printed, so you can see if it is economical to produce a few more while you are at it.)

**Colour:** This could be any number of colours if you are using 'spot' colour (i.e. special individual inks that give you a precise colour). You may go for black and white, or black and white plus another colour. You may use the four colour process (magenta, cyan, yellow, black ink – 'cmyk' – are mixed together to form other colours). Through cmyk you can reproduce colour photographs. The colours often end up less vibrant than printing using individual spot colour inks.

**Paper weight:** This is normally specified in gsm. 90gsm and below feels quite 'throw away' and lightweight. At 150gsm you start to feel that a document is good quality. Ask for samples to help you decide

**Paper type:** You might specify a percentage of recycled fibre content or ask for paper that has come from sustainably managed forests. Ask for background information and for any industry kitemarks that support a claim that paper has an environmental pedigree.

**Finish:** You might go for a matt or gloss finish (a smooth flat silky finish or more of a shiny look). Brochures might be glued, stapled or stitched.

**Collation:** If you have loose-leaf inserts you might want them collated in a certain way.

**Lamination:** If appropriate you might want the document sealed and protected in laminate.

# 4

# Websites

This chapter looks at how campaigners and fundraisers can use websites to help promote a cause. We do not cover the technical details, but we look at the content and structure of an effective site, how to attract people to visit, and the processes involved in producing a site.

**This chapter will give you some ideas on how to:**

▶ develop a website that will be a useful promotional tool;
▶ ensure people visit the site.

## Register your name

If you are planning a website now or in the future, then register the name you want to use – the 'domain name' (this is the bit that comes after www.). There is an organisation called Nominet UK which registers addresses for the Internet in the United Kingdom. You pay a fee and buy the appropriate address or addresses for your organisation. You can go direct to Nominet (www.nominet.net). There are other organisations that buy and sell domain names. Some will do you a bargain deal if you use their computers to 'host' or house your website (paying them, of course, to do so). Other organisations have registered a number of names they think people may want in the future in the hope that they will get a lot of money in return.

## Coming up with content and a structure

Before you begin work on your site, take some time to have a look at what other organisations have done. The great thing about the Internet is that you can do a vast amount of research from your desk. Make a note of the sites you like and try to identify what it is that appeals: the speed with which you can load the site, the design, the interactivity and so on. If you are asking someone else to help you create the site then they will find it very helpful to have some examples of what you are trying to achieve or what you definitely want to avoid.

Visit the website www.fundraising.co.uk There are a number of useful links, but more importantly it has a wealth of ideas about how to use the web to raise funds. Also visit www.co-financing.co.uk for hints on various sources of funding.

Pick out some key words relating to your particular area of concern. Search the Internet to find out what already exists. Make a note of those sites you would like to link up to so that people can be directed from one site to another. Look in particular for more general sites that are likely to be quite popular because it is important you attract people to your website in as many ways as possible.

## Working with a web designer

If you do not have the time or expertise in-house and want to employ a web designer then there are various ways you can find them. If you look in your Yellow Pages you will find some listed under Internet Web Design. Ask them for examples of sites so that you can have a browse and see if you like what they have to offer.

You can also search the Internet for 'web+designers'. You might want to restrict such a search to your local area by adding that into your search. Again, take a look at some of the sites they have already designed to see if you feel happy with their approach.

You might also have some favourite sites already. Find out from the organisation concerned whether or not the site was designed in-house or by an external company. If a web designer was contracted, ask them how easy the person or organisation was to work with. Personal recommendations count for a lot, but this is an area where the designer's wares are on display.

## Be clear about what you want

There is always new technology coming along, allowing you to add whistles and bells to a website. Many web designers are keen to try it out, so be clear about what you want included in your site and what you want it to be able to do. If a designer offers you new technical solutions always ask if there is a different (and cheaper) solution available.

# Producing something worthwhile and relevant

As a fundraiser or campaigner, you do not want your website to just sit there giving out a bit of information about your organisation. You want to create something dynamic that will prompt people to take some sort of action.

Here are some of the elements that you might include in your site. You can mix and match and adapt as suits your particular organisation.

## Home page

This is where people arrive when they first visit your site.

- You can opt for simplicity and limit the number of pictures on the page so that it is quick and easy to load. You have probably tried to visit some sites and given up because the home page takes so long to appear on your screen.
- If you think people will be prepared to wait for the page to load, and you have the resources to update the page regularly, you might want to have a home page which features a news update. This helps to ensure people will not be bored with your site.
- You might include a contents list or menu on your home page. Alternatively, you might simply have a welcome message and a button to click to enter the site.
- You might also include a counter to show how many people have visited the site, a note of when the page or site was last updated and other devices to reassure people that they are visiting a popular and well maintained website.

## General information

You might have a section that gives a bit of history to your organisation and answers some 'frequently asked questions'. In this section define the work that your organisation does and some of the terms that you use throughout the site, to help those less familiar with your organisation.

## Get in touch

Make it easy for people to contact you. Many otherwise excellent websites seem to have hidden contact details. Not only is it important to give e-mail details and a form for people to respond on, it is also worth giving conventional phone, fax and postal details.

## Message board

If you are running a campaign then you will want to know if any of your supporters are involved in particular activities, have comments to share, or want to get in touch with others. A message board means that they get something valuable from your site and will hopefully visit it regularly. Fundraisers can also use message boards to good effect if you have volunteers raising money in different areas. They can share ideas and successes on the site, so encouraging others. You probably will not want to check all messages as they go onto the board before they appear. But you will need to look at the board once a day to ensure no inappropriate messages appear.

## Searchable databases

Many people use the Internet to find things out and are used to searching on sites. This is done through a database of information. The user types in key words and the database finds relevant details. If you have a number of reports and publications then a search button will help people find relevant information.

A regional voluntary organisation has included a searchable database of projects on its website. This means that people can find out what local charities are doing in their area or in their field of interest. They decided to use a database rather than a menu with lots of items in it so that people could find their way round the site more easily.

An international development agency uses a database to store information on merchandise that people can buy online. The web coordinator felt more comfortable promoting goods in this way, rather than having a 'shop window' within the site with products permanently on display.

A voluntary sector development agency lists key organisations, politicians and others that supporters would want to lobby as part of a campaign. The details listed are in the public domain and those included have given their consent.

## Chatroom

Unless you are going to employ a fulltime moderator you probably will not want to set up a live chatroom that is available 24 hours a day, seven days a week. However, you might want to have the facility to use a chatroom for particular occasions: at the launch of a campaign; when a key politician is visiting; when you want to do some planning with volunteers who are spread out over a wide geographical area.

## Games and activities

Your website does not have to be packed full of serious information. You can include something a bit more lighthearted to attract people. Quizzes and activities can be used to educate, whilst still being fun.

A conservation charity has included an area of fun activities for young people within its website. It also has plans for a virtual 'club' for children. This has helped the organisation to reach a new and loyal audience.

## Resources

A website is an ideal place to share good practice and actual materials that people can use. You can store downloadable leaflets and presentation aids. You are providing people with a valuable resource but at the same time you are ensuring they give out the messages you want.

## Links

Include links to other relevant sites, and ask if the links can be reciprocal.

## News

You can use your site to publish your newsletter and other information about current events and activities.

## Research

You can use your site to help gather information about people's opinions, habits and beliefs. The findings can be published to help publicise the site.

## On-line sales and auctions

You might want a part of the site to be dedicated to direct fundraising activities. The money could be generated through on-line auctions (which involve as much effort as any other auction and have to be managed carefully). Another option is to have an on-line sales catalogue, offering different items of merchandise for sale. To run such an operation you need to firstly ensure that your organisation is set up to trade in this way. You will also need to have your site based on a secure server if you are taking on-line credit card details. You also need to have a system in place to handle the response required.

# Users with disabilities

Try to keep your page layouts simple. You can check whether or not they are accessible for disabled users by running a programme called 'Bobby'. This gives you a rating for your site and highlights any problems with accessibility – those things that you need to adjust to make the site accessible, such as including descriptions of the graphics you use. The Employers Forum on Disability has produced a guide with advice on developing accessible websites. The RNIB also provides helpful guidance. See *Further information* on p111.

# Advertising

Some sites sell advertising space. If you already have funders that advertise in your printed material then they might want to support you online. You might also include a 'plaque' on specific areas, like those you see on theatre seats and park benches, thanking a person or organisation for their kind donation.

# Testing and development

When you have some ideas about what you want to include in your site you will need to capture this and plan the construction.

The first thing to do is to map out a structure. Use a flow chart to show the different levels. You will have a home page at the top, and then at the next level you will have a series of pages that introduce different main sections. Each of these will sub-divide further into other pages.

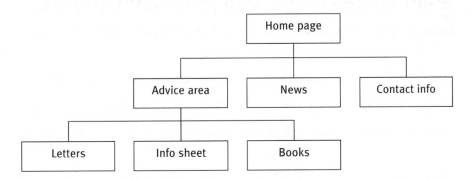

If you want to test out different elements of the site before you launch it fully, then you could set it up with its own web address (if you are using a web designer then they will have a number of spare addresses for work in development). You can give this address to a group of people that will test out the site. When you are satisfied that it is working properly it can be moved to its official address.

## Maintenance

Before you launch your site you need to ensure you can keep it up to date. If people will be visiting and leaving messages, you need someone to review them. If you are offering a live chat room then you will need a moderator. If you want people to come again to your site, then you will need to refresh what is on there. This means having someone with at least part of their job dedicated to maintaining the site. If you do not build this into your planning then the initial investment in the site is more or less wasted.

# Attracting people to the site

Your website is a valuable promotional tool, but if you do not 'sell' it then no one will visit. Here are some of the ways you could attract people to your site.

- Register your site with the various Internet search engines, providing key words and phrases.
- Search for sites that might offer a link to your own.
- Organise a launch event to attract local media coverage.
- Publish the results of a survey on the site and then publicise the survey. The aim is to get an article in a newspaper that refers people on to the site.
- Run a competition on the site and send out flyers promoting it.
- Produce postcards and bookmarks highlighting the web address.
- Include the web address on your letterhead and in your e-mails.

# Main stages in the web production process

**Research:** Find out what sites you like and what people would like from your website.

**Storyboard:** Construct a flowchart to show the different elements in your site.

**Design concept:** Come up with an overall look and feel for the site.

**Name main areas:** Devise names for the main elements in the site. Then buttons or a contents list can be developed.

**Write copy:** Write all the introductory material, instructions, help notes, and so on.

**Supply illustrations:** Provide pictures to illustrate the site.

**Supply materials:** Provide downloadable materials.

**Programming:** You or a webmaster will programme all the material so that it can be read through standard web browsing software.

**Testing:** Run the site on a separate address and invite feedback from a limited group. Amend before moving to the main site.

**Launch:** Promote the website to your supporters and more widely through the media.

**Maintenance:** Ensure someone has a clearly defined role to maintain and update the site.

# Setting a budget

Your website budget should include the following elements:

- project management time – to research and develop the ideas;
- registration of the domain name – making sure that your web address is registered and unique to your organisation;
- design and programming – designing the overall look and feel of the site, coming up with a structure, and programming the contents;
- website hosting – you will need to buy the space on which your website is located;
- maintenance – employing someone to keep your site up to date;
- promotion – to attract people to the site.

# 5

# Video and audio

In this section we look at how video and audio cassettes might help you to promote your cause. We explain some of the techniques that you might employ in a tape to ensure you keep your audience and encourage them to take action. We outline the main stages involved in the creation of a tape and explain how to set a budget.

**After reading this chapter you will know:**

▶ when it is appropriate to use a tape to promote your cause;
▶ the different strengths of videos and audios;
▶ some of the rules to follow if you are making a tape to promote your cause;
▶ how to commission and produce a cassette;
▶ the distribution options open to you;
▶ how to budget for a production.

## When and how to use video

Videos can be used in a number of ways and you need to anticipate how they will be watched. This will influence exactly what goes into the video itself and how it is packaged. Here are some of the ways in which you may use a video to help promote your cause.

## Presentation

A video could form part of your presentation at conferences and seminars. You would always be there to introduce it and pull out the key points. Such a video could simply feature some powerful case studies. It might document a project or include a message from someone who cannot be with you. You might show a clip from a longer video. The video might be an inspirational montage of images from different projects. You probably will not want anything longer than five minutes in this setting.

# Exhibition

You might produce a video to use at exhibitions, which could be played when there is no one there to talk about it. The video has to stand on its own. Such exhibition videos are ideally quite short, probably up to a maximum of 10 minutes long so that people can drop by your stand and watch them comfortably. If you are showing a video at an exhibition and want people to take action then there really should be a member of staff on hand at all times. If not, ensure there are plenty of leaflets around or forms for people to pick up and sign.

# Training

A video can be used to train other people. Fundraisers might want to provide information to volunteers who are involved in raising money from the general public. Campaigners might want to educate volunteers about work that is going on elsewhere in the country or world.

# Via other agencies

You might produce a video that is disseminated to the public through other agencies. Environmental campaigners, for instance, might make a video available through Local Agenda 21 officers, based in local councils. You have entrusted them to pass the video to the right kind of people and to introduce it in the right context. But you will need to make sure that the video can stand alone, just in case.

# Individual viewing

In a similar way if you are sending out a video for individuals to view on their own – at home or in the office – then the project needs to be self-explanatory. You may consider producing the video on CD or DVD depending on the audience you are trying to reach.

# What videos are good for

Videos are particularly good at:

- conveying emotion;
- inspiring and motivating the audience;
- demonstrating how things can work through real life examples;
- allowing people to learn by example or from their peers.

## Uses of video

Fundraisers and campaigners can use video to:

- show people problems and solutions;
- change the way people feel about an issue;
- urge people to take action or donate money (those who could benefit from this support might make a direct appeal for help).

# When and how to use audio

A promotional audio cassette will probably be used in one of two contexts:

**In the car:** In this case your audience might listen to the tape in small chunks, over a number of journeys. You can help by dividing the tape into easily consumable sections.

**At home:** Someone listening to a tape at home is more likely to hear the whole thing in one sitting.

You could consider producing an audio CD as well as or instead of a cassette but if you expect people to listen in chunks, a cassette is easier to manipulate because a CD will always return to the beginning when you switch it off.

Audio tapes are particularly good at:

- encouraging the audience to use their imagination;
- presenting information from anonymous case studies;
- delivering more detailed information than video, because attention is focused on what is being said.

Fundraisers and campaigners can use audio tapes to:

- share case studies, while protecting the participants' confidentiality;
- put across more complex information about their cause;
- appeal directly for them to take action or donate money.

# Creating something that grabs and holds attention

However you intend to use your video or audio cassette, it is essential to grab the audience's attention and then hold it for the rest of the programme. Here are some ways in which you can get people to watch or listen.

- Start with a quote or piece of action that captures the essence of the programme. Alternatively begin with an intriguing quote or piece of action that will leave the audience wanting to know more.

- Explain early on what the programme sets out to achieve. You can do this through a title sequence, a voice-over, a presenter, or caption. Even if the tape is found without its box or packaging the audience should quickly know what they have put into their player.

- Use appropriate music to create a mood and help punctuate the programme. There is now some excellent library music available so that your production does not have to end up like a corporate video from the Seventies. There are a lot of companies issuing library music on CD; they advertise in magazines such as *Broadcast* (see *Further information* on p111). If you are working with a production company they will be able to find the right kind of music. You will need to make a payment for using the music. The amount payable depends on where and how you will use the cassette. You pay more if you get it cleared for all eventualities. However, if you get clearance for a tape to be made available for hire or rental by individuals and then you are asked by a broadcaster if they can use it you will have to go through the process again and pay extra.

- If your programme is longer than 15 minutes, divide it into sections and use a device such as a repeated burst of music or fade to black/silence to mark the sections. This will help to keep people interested and if they do have to switch off they can tune back in more easily.

- Use real life examples, quotes from people and people involved in their everyday lives as much as possible. It brings all the theory and preaching to life.

An advocate working with young disadvantaged people helped them to create an audio tape aimed at local government officials and councillors. The young people called the production 'Mirror, Signal, Listen' and included instructions to play the tape in the car. Five young people were featured on the tape. Each introduced themselves and began by describing their current position in work, training, learning, volunteering, and so on. Then they went on to explain how and why they had been excluded from school, how they felt about this, and how they thought things might change for the better.

At the end one of the young people talked about the title of the tape. It was not just because the listeners were driving as the tape played: 'Look in the *mirror* – you were young like us; send us a *signal* that you care about us; really *listen* to us.'

# Including opportunities to respond

You want people to take action. You do not just want them to watch a video or listen to a cassette and say, 'That's nice!' So, what can you do to ensure they respond in some way?

Here are some ideas.

# Present the programme personally

If you are in the room when the programme has been played then you can encourage the audience to tell you what they think, and ultimately take some kind of action. It is best to discuss the programme a bit first rather than plunging straight in there asking for money or for people to sign up to a campaign. In talking things through you will find out some useful feedback, different members of the audience will start to influence others and you have the opportunity for ideas to emerge from the group about how to take things forward. If someone in the audience asks how they can do more to help then this is a very positive way of encouraging others to volunteer too. It is, of course, much more rewarding than going in with a hard sell.

## Include a reply-paid leaflet, web address or phoneline

You could include a leaflet and stamped addressed envelope/reply-paid envelope. Alternatively you might promote a web address or phone number for further action. As well as giving details within the video or audio you could include a reference in the cassette packaging too. Be very direct within the tape about what people should do next. In videos use both voice and text.

## Offer something else

If you think it will help, offer people something in return for making contact. For instance, you might say, 'Phone now and pledge your support and we'll send you a Save the Hospital T-shirt.'

# Main stages in the video/audio production process

You may decide to produce a tape yourself or, more usually, you will commission a production company. The stages involved in the development of the programme will be the same.

## Develop a programme brief

It is worth doing this even if you are producing a programme in-house so that everyone is clear about what is being created. It will also help you to set a budget for those elements you will still need to buy in, e.g. packaging, duplication, distribution. The brief should outline:

- the overall purpose or aim of the programme;
- the target audience;
- the way in which the programme will be used (in what context);
- ideas on who might be featured in the programme or how much research will be needed to find them;
- a timetable with a deadline for the delivery of a master tape and another final deadline for the duplicated tapes;
- information on accessibility (whether or not you are producing a version with sub-titles, in sign language, and in other community languages);
- the available budget (if you want to reveal such information);

- an outline of what is required from a company that wants to submit a tender (i.e. whether you want a detailed description of the suggested programme content, timetable, budget, samples of previous work, and so on).

# Begin research

Even if you are already know who will take part someone needs to spend time with them in advance of the recording. They need to know what to expect, and the producer needs to know what they are likely to say. Further research is also needed into the places (locations) where the programme will be recorded.

# Pre-production

You might want to know the likely structure of the programme before the video is shot or the audio recorded. This is helpful but it is no guarantee of what you will end up with (which will hopefully be much better).

# Production

If you have commissioned an external production company you will probably want to go along to at least some of the recording to ensure everything is going to plan. There appears to be lots of waiting around, but actually it is time well spent because the sound person may be getting the levels absolutely right so that you end up with a top quality programme; the director may be waiting for the right lighting conditions; or the camera operator may be ensuring the interviewee looks relaxed.

Ensure all participants sign 'release forms', which mean they are happy for you to use their contribution and edit as appropriate. Explain how the tape might be used. If you get clearance from them for it to be used as a video but not broadcast you will have to go back to them again should you want to screen it in this way. It therefore makes sense to get clearance to use it as widely as possible.

# Post-production

There are a number of stages to be gone through after the recording. The producer will review all the tapes, compare this with the original plans and come up with a 'paper edit', which knits together the most relevant pieces. It is a paper edit because it is all simply cut and paste on paper before going into an edit suite. It is your golden opportunity to check you are happy with progress before money is spent on editing.

Video editing is done in two stages: the offline and online. The offline puts together the pieces of video in the right order, includes a few of the special effects that will be used in the final programme, but is all done at a lower quality than the online. Once the offline is tweaked and approved the video is put together finally in the online. The sound is dubbed (adjusted and smoothed out) and the video is ready as a master for duplication.

## Music licence

You need to get a licence from the Mechanical Copyright Protection Service (MCPS, see *Further information* on p112) to use any library music in a programme. There is a fee to be paid.

## Other languages and subtitles for video

Once you have your master tape you can produce other slightly different versions. You can produce a copy with subtitles. You can add a sign language interpreter, and you can dub the video into other community languages.

## Duplication and packaging

Before you send a master tape off to be copied make sure you have a safety copy just in case anything should happen to your master. You may have already come up with a design for the packaging of the cassette, but sometimes it pays to wait so that the cover can reflect the style of the contents.

# Setting a budget

The main elements of a programme budget are:

- project management time (yours);
- research, producer, director (the production company if you commission an outside agency);
- production crew and tapes;
- travel and subsistence during the production;
- facility fees: a contribution to any locations used;
- post-production: the editor, edit suite, tapes, dubbing, music;
- design, print and production of packaging;
- duplication of tapes;
- distribution.

# 6

# Using the media

In this chapter we look at some of the ways you can work with the media to help promote your cause. Turn to almost any newspaper, tune in to almost any television or radio station and you will find stories about community organisations. The good thing is that very often they are positive about the organisation concerned. We explore some of the main opportunities for getting your message across to a mass audience.

**After reading this chapter you will know how to:**

▶ spot a news story or create a news angle;
▶ write a news/press release;
▶ approach the media with confidence;
▶ get the most out of an interview on radio or television;
▶ target people through specialist outlets.

## The changing face of the media

Those of us who enjoy a daily dose of the 'Today' programme, while we eat our breakfast and read our broadsheet can still do so. But, if we feel so inclined, we can also log on to the Internet to watch Radio 4's presenters put politicians through their paces and then surf a newspaper site to find out about what stories are breaking, and search old ones in the archive. Before we look at some of the techniques you can use to get publicity for your cause let us take a quick tour through some of the recent changes to the media. In each case we highlight how this might be relevant for fundraisers and campaigners.

## Very local radio companies

In recent years a whole wave of new local radio stations have been awarded licences to broadcast. They are focused on very local areas, often a single town or city and its immediate surroundings. They are committed to providing very local information and news, often adding to and changing news bulletins up to 30 times each day. You may find that these smaller local stations are more prepared than the larger independent commercial stations to get actively involved in campaigns. Even if they do not participate they are likely to offer you an interview opportunity if you are launching, or have good news about, a campaign.

## Very local television companies

A number of smaller television companies has been launched even more recently than the small local radio stations. Some welcome video footage from community groups. Others produce their own material, but are particularly interested in hearing about local community activity. Check first with your local station to see if it wants material, find out what tape format is preferred and then consider investing in a digital video camera. You might find that your material is frequently used, but you will need to make a judgement about the effort involved and the number of people you are likely to reach.

## Digital cable and satellite television channels

If you receive cable or satellite you will be aware of the hundreds of channels to choose from. Not all will be appropriate for fundraisers and campaigners, but some of the news and lifestyle channels might be relevant. Do not forget to include Sky News in your list of media to be sent press releases.

Fundraisers and campaigners can work with the Community Channel to publicise their cause. It is a channel dedicated to raising awareness of social issues and encouraging community action. There are also some channels focusing on health, money and women that might be relevant for your campaigns. If you are making a video and you think that it might be used in its entirety on a satellite channel make sure you get clearances from participants and from the MCPS (for music).

> A campaigner commissioned a video about a child health issue, to be distributed through health visitors and clinics. Then a month after the video was launched a satellite channel asked if it could transmit the programme. All the participants had signed release forms giving permission for them to be shown in a video or on television (via satellite). However, the music had only been cleared for use in a video. The extra cost of clearing the music for satellite broadcast was £1,000.

# News websites

Most national and local newspapers have an online version, often with additional information and facilities. But there are also local community websites that only exist on the Internet and are never published on paper. Find out if there is one for your area; visit www.touchoxford.com for an example. Such sites include local community news, and should welcome news releases and photographs.

## An idea for campaigners and fundraisers

Set up a joint Internet-based campaign with a newspaper that has an online section or with a web-based news organisation. You could have a semi-permanent place on the site, listed in the main menu so that local people can find out how things are going and perhaps get involved themselves. As you promote the initiative you attract people to the site. As people visit the site they come across your campaign.

# Online journalists

Programmes and individual journalists encourage e-mail contact and responses. Some programmes finish broadcasting and then continue with online chat rooms. They feed back comments in their next edition. There is, then, an opportunity to respond instantly if you hear something on the radio or want to comment on a TV or newspaper article. There is also, increasingly, a chance to correspond directly with a relevant journalist who might never have returned your phone calls in the past. Fundraisers and campaigners could build up e-mail address books of journalists interested in their area of work.

You should also agree a protocol with colleagues of how to represent the organisation if taking part in a chatroom or responding by e-mail to a programme. Given the speed with which the medium works it is probably impractical for such e-mails to be run through an approval process. You therefore need to decide in what circumstances individuals are speaking on their own behalf or for the organisation. Decide whether or not to include a disclaimer at the bottom of all your e-mails to say that the views of an individual do not necessarily reflect those of the whole organisation.

## The continuing importance of conventional media

Having said all that about new and emerging media opportunities it is worth stressing the continued importance of the more conventional media: newspapers (national and local); specialist magazines; radio (national and local); and television (national and local). All have quite large and (relatively) loyal audiences and offer you an opportunity to reach a high number of people with your messages.

# Spotting a news angle

The most common way in which community organisations promote their cause through the media is in the news. You therefore need to be able to identify what it is that you are doing that could be considered newsworthy.

Below we list some of the things that a journalist might consider newsworthy. We have left out references to sex, disasters and fraud. These ingredients would be very newsworthy but you probably would not be glad of the ensuing publicity. Instead we have focused on some of the things that you might be able to come up with to promote your cause.

## Launches and firsts

If you are starting something new then this is newsworthy, particularly if it is the first of its kind in the local area. You are more likely to get coverage if you do something to mark the launch. Ribbon-cutting and unveiling ceremonies are a bit over-done. You might involve a celebrity to help add to the newsworthiness. Alternatively focus on an 'ordinary' individual who is the first to benefit from your new service, the first to change their behaviour because of your campaign, or the first to respond to your appeal.

When you launch a campaign consider featuring an individual as a case study: someone who is going to benefit from your service or someone who needs your support. Of course they need to be willing to participate, but focusing on a strong personal story can hit home.

## Celebrities and VIPs

We mentioned celebrities above. They might help to highlight a launch, but they might also simply visit a project to raise awareness of your cause. Make sure they are well informed if you work with them in this way, because it is the celebrity that journalists will want to interview rather than your chief executive.

A well-known actor who has given a lot of time to a particular charity agreed to help promote a new campaign which included a website giving interactive advice. They agreed to a live radio interview as they were in the town performing in a play. Everything went well until they were asked for the website address – and did not know where to direct people.

## Surveys and statistics

Journalists respond well to surveys that can be expressed fairly easily: 'One in six of us . . .' If you are sending a news release to a local journalist then you need to highlight the statistics that are relevant to their area, indicating whether this is above or below average. If you issue a news release about a survey ensure it is based on a robust report, because journalists will often ask for a more detailed document in support of the story. So, even if you conduct the survey yourself, make sure there is a written report that explains who was surveyed, what methods were used, and the headline results.

You can make good use of this approach to raise awareness of a cause: perhaps four in ten people are likely to be affected by a health problem, yet only one in ten of us is likely to be treated for the condition; perhaps less than one in ten local shops is accessible for disabled people; perhaps only 20% of local schoolchildren has access to an after school club compared with the national average of X%. Campaigners and fundraisers can use such a statistic to introduce the idea and then follow up by explaining how we can do something to change the situation.

## A perspective on another story

Essentially, this means giving your thoughts on someone else's news. If you are aware that a story is about to break that is relevant to your organisation then you can prepare something in advance. Otherwise you have to be ready to move into action once you hear the first news reports of the day.

For instance, a story comes out about national crime statistics, highlighting the likelihood of young people being involved in crime (as perpetrators or victims). If you are a group that offers support to young people at risk then you might want to draw attention to your work by: sending in a letter or e-mail; issuing a release that incorporates a quote referring to the crime report and going on to highlight the good practice you are involved in; launching a new project to coincide with the news; or drawing attention to a forthcoming event at which people will address these issues.

## An amazing milestone

Is your organisation nearing its 10th, 50th or 100th anniversary? If it is then the media may well be interested. But it is not just birthdays that make for newsworthy milestones. The 100th person to benefit from your work, the 1,000th volunteer to come forward, the 100,000th call to your helpline: all these are milestones worthy of coverage in local media.

## Fundraising success (or failure)

When you succeed in raising money, this is something the media are normally happy to celebrate with you. The bigger the amount of funding and the more significant the work that will result, the more likely you are to receive coverage. Having said that, the amount of column inches does not always reflect the size of the grant, though. You can also get publicity if your bid for funding is turned down and you think this was unfair. If a journalist knows of your organisation's work and senses this is under threat because funding has been turned down they will want to run a story calling for a change of mind or another funder to step in.

## Forthcoming event

Some media run special sections listing forthcoming events. You might also be able to get a mention in the news if you can draw attention to what is most interesting about the event, such as an international speaker or a fascinating topic.

## A good photo opportunity

Obviously this does not apply to radio, but if you have something happening that will make a great photo or shot for television, this can be sufficient to tempt the media along. It is always worth having a back-up photographer of your own in case no one comes and also to have shots you can send to other papers.

When you send out a release inviting people to a photo opportunity, spell out what will be going on. Do not just say 'badminton demonstrations' or even 'badminton demonstrations by the Sorted Club'. Instead say 'Badminton demonstrations by the Sorted Club: young disabled people aged 8–11 years will play a mini-tournament. Local MP Brian Smith will present the winners' trophies.' Provide detailed timings for the various elements. Based on this information an editor can decide to send a photographer or camera person along to capture the tournament as it is being played, wait and join the event when the trophies are being presented, or arrange to come along at the end to 'mock up' some action shots.

## A forceful comment

You might issue a release condemning something or calling for action. Alternatively you might issue a release in which you are praised by an authority. Either way if the comment is strongly worded you are likely to get coverage.

For instance, you might issue a release in which your chief executive says, 'It is an absolute disgrace that nothing has been done to help.' This is more likely to be picked up by journalists than a release in which your boss says, 'We want more to be done to help.' If you have been praised by an independent funder, evaluator or inspector this is more likely to get coverage if they say, 'This is an absolutely outstanding project that deserves to go from strength to strength,' than if they say, 'This project is good.'

## Heroes and heroines

If you are responsible for saving something from destruction, rescuing someone from the brink then this should receive publicity. The more unusual the circumstances the more likely it is that you will get coverage.

## No guarantees

Remember that you will always be competing with hundreds of other news stories and there is limited space available. You might come up with something that on paper sounds extremely newsworthy and which you care about a great deal. But if something more dramatic and of interest to more people reading that newspaper, listening to that station, or watching that programme, comes up then your story will be edged out.

## Making contact

The essential tool in making contact with the media is a press release or – more friendly to radio and television – the news release. You can post it, fax it or e-mail it. However you send it (and we will discuss the options below) you first have to write it.

# The format of a news release

There are some basic conventions that are frequently used in setting out news releases.

## Use a logo

The news release is issued on paper with the organisation's logo. It may not go out on your letterhead if you are issuing a release jointly with another organisation. Essentially, a journalist should be able to know at a glance where the story is coming from.

## Tell them it is a news release

The heading 'news', 'news release' or 'press release' normally appears somewhere on the paper, just to confirm that it is what it looks like.

## Give a date

Somewhere prominent (usually just above or below the heading) is the date. The date might be the date of issue, or it might be the embargo date. An 'embargo' allows you to issue a release in advance of the news being officially out in the open. This gives a journalist time to prepare the story without leaking it in advance. It usually works.

## Use a catchline

If your release runs over more than one page then put a 'catchline' in the top left hand corner. The word or words should succinctly reflect the story. If, for instance, your release is about the lack of appropriate care in residential homes for gay and lesbian older people your catchline might be 'older gay care'. Then you say this is page 1 of 2 or 1 of 3. The catchline appears on all other pages with the appropriate page number. That way it is obvious if for any reason the pages become detached, and the release can be easily put together again.

## Keep the heading simple

The main heading is normally punchy and straightforward. Do not try to make a pun, leave it to the journalists. The danger of trying to be clever and funny is that someone on the receiving end misses the point and runs an inaccurate story.

## Tell them when it is over

At the bottom of each page write 'more' if the release continues or 'ends' if that is all there is.

### Who can give more information

At the end of the release include contact details for further information. The person listed should be aware that their name and number is being given out to the media and they should be available to respond.

### Provide notes

You might provide further notes for journalists who might not be aware of the background on your organisation and your work.

# Writing a news release

When writing a news release you should follow the tips for effective writing outlined in the chapter on *Printed material* on p24. Keep sentences and words short. Avoid jargon. Assume nothing.

Think of the structure of a news release as being a triangle. At the top is the most important information provided in brief. The first paragraph is a single sentence, possibly two sentences. The next paragraph provides some further information. The paragraph below adds to the first two and so on. A sub-editor should be able to draw a line after any of the paragraphs and the story should still make sense.

### The first paragraph – think bus stop

The first paragraph should sum up the news you want to publicise. It is a single sentence of probably no more than 20 words. To help you focus on making it punchy imagine yourself at a bus stop. Your friend is just getting on to the bus and it is pulling away. As this happens you shout, 'Oh, by the way, did you know . . .', and your first paragraph follows.

For instance, if a well-known footballer was going to launch your new playscheme for children with learning disabilities you would not shout:

> Next Thursday the Bollingshire PlayLearn Group which has been running for 10 years is launching a new scheme that will be of immense benefit to young people with learning disabilities and their siblings. The launch will start with a party for the children and then there will be a game of football which will be joined by local football captain David Standham . . .

No, you would declare:

> David Standham's launching our new play scheme next week. Isn't that brilliant?

And your news release would probably be something along the lines of:

> Bollingshire United captain David Standham will launch a new playscheme for local charity Bollingshire PlayLearn next Thursday.

## The second paragraph – think news in brief

Now you elaborate on the first paragraph to give some further information. If you remember that this paragraph together with the first might be all that is used for a 'news in brief' item it will help you keep to the essentials.

> The new playscheme will help young people with learning disabilities by providing sports activities, social outings and learning opportunities. The scheme has received a three year grant from the Community Fund.

The piece could finish here and it would make perfect sense. But it would be nice now to hear from someone connected with the project or – even better – from David Standham

## The third paragraph – think quote

Try not to use a bland quote that is safe but boring. If you want the quote to be used it needs to build on what goes before, adding information if possible.

> 'We're thrilled that after five years of fundraising this scheme is finally getting off the ground,' says Jane Taupin, the group's chairperson. 'We have been able to offer playschemes to many children in Bollingshire over the past 10 years, but we haven't had the trained staff to help young people with learning disabilities. Now we have funding for the next three years and we're already fundraising furiously to keep the scheme going into the future.'

From this quote we have learnt quite a bit more about the group and it is said in a nice personal way. If the quote came from David Standham it might be a little different:

> 'I'm delighted to help kickstart this scheme,' says local football star David Standham. 'The group's volunteers have shown remarkable dedication, spending the last five years raising the money to get the scheme off the ground. They are well known for their innovative and friendly playschemes for children from mainstream backgrounds. But until now they haven't had the trained staff to help young people with learning difficulties. The funding's now in place and I'm looking forward to its continued success.'

We learn the same amount of information about the group, but it gains a little star quality if it is attributed to the local celebrity. Of course you would probably make the quote up and then ask him if it was all right to say he had said it, but this is the way it normally works.

### The fourth paragraph – think action

After giving out most of the details you should move on to how the audience can get involved. This might mean giving a phone number and often it helps if this is included in a quote. In our news release we might include the following:

> The group wants to hear from parents of young people with learning disabilities aged 0–12 years who might benefit. Chairperson Jane Taupin says: 'Now that the scheme is up and running we want to help as many young people as possible. We've got up to 20 places available each weekend. We are particularly keen to hear from parents who have managed with no outside support in the past. They deserve a break and I urge them to ring 0132.'

### The fifth paragraph – think nice but not necessary

The next paragraph or two will give further information but probably will not be used. If there is room they will go in; if space is tight they will be cut. Our final paragraph might say:

> Bollingshire PlayLearn is based in the Green House in Flint Road. It aims to make a difference to local children's lives through creative and integrated play.

### More information

If you have too much information to fit into five paragraphs think in terms of sections. The first section would still be the short one sentence paragraph. Then further sections might be two paragraphs or more, but following the same sort of structure through to the fifth 'nice but not necessary' section.

# Sending out your release

You have three main options as to how you send your news release. You can post it, fax it, e-mail it. Postage can be expensive, but it you are sending a release to a wide range of media it might be the most convenient approach. It also means that a piece of paper lands on the desk as part of the morning routine of the newsdesk. You are pretty safe in the knowledge that it has actually arrived. Faxing is good for speed. It again ensures a piece of paper lands on someone's desk for consideration. It is also cheaper than postage. E-mail is quick and cheap and can help you build up a personal relationship with a journalist if you have their direct address. However, you may have a nagging doubt as to whether or not the e-mail has arrived, been picked up by the right person and printed off.

If you have the time it is worth first ringing up the relevant journalist, saying you are going to send over details and ask them how they would prefer to receive the information. That way you have alerted them to the potential news item and they will hopefully recognise it when it arrives – and be more receptive to what you have sent.

Follow up phone calls are useful if you are organising an event and want to know if journalists plan to attend. Newsdesks can get fed up with people calling up to chase a news release so do it gently. If a newspaper tells you no one is coming along, ask them if they would like a photo anyway. If a radio station cannot make it, offer them a down-the-line interview. There is no point in being too pushy. Sometimes a story will grab their interest, sometimes it will not. If you push too hard on something they do not want to use you will find it harder to convince them to use something more interesting in the future.

# Speaking to journalists

If you send out a news release you must be prepared to talk to journalists who ring up and want to know more. If they phone for a quote and it is not a convenient moment, ask them for a deadline and promise to ring them back at an agreed time. Make sure you stick to that time.

If they want to come and talk to you, again agree a mutually convenient time. Find out how long they will have before they arrive. Ask if they would like you to arrange a suitable photo opportunity.

In the course of your interview they might ask you questions that seem slightly off the point. Usually they are simply searching for an angle and exploring whether there is a different approach to the one suggested in your news release. If you are worried that the questions sound negative then try not to simply give 'yes' or 'no' responses. Be prepared to go into detail to explain the complexity of a situation. If they ask difficult questions then they should be prepared to spend time on understanding the issues.

# Photo opportunities

Sometimes a striking picture will be sufficient reason for a newspaper to cover a story. If you want a national newspaper to run a picture then it has to be stunning. Study the national papers to which you might want to send a photograph. *The Guardian*, for instance, runs lots of pictures that are highly artistic, featuring repetition/patterns. To get a picture of high enough quality you might need to commission a freelance press photographer.

If you are setting up a photo opportunity, then it is worth spelling out just what the photo will contain when you send out your press invite. Handshake and cheque presentation pictures are clichés, but they do still appear frequently. Try to be a bit more adventurous. Here are a few tips:

### Involve children

If it is appropriate then children enliven a photo. They are generally much more active and smiley than adults. Ensure you have the permission of a parent or guardian before involving them in the picture.

### Make it active

Come up with a photo that will feature action. It is more natural than a static group shot. It can help to tell a story, which a head and shoulders picture of your chief executive cannot achieve. Involve any special guests or celebrities in your action shot.

### Make it fun

Setting up a photo opportunity is all very staged. You should approach it light heartedly and be willing to join in the fun.

### Branding

Take the opportunity to get your organisation's logo or a campaign's branding into a photo. Photographers will normally be cooperative about this. You might use a banner, hard hat (if you are working on a building project), T-shirts, exhibition panel, baseball caps. Be bold enough to ensure the logo comes out clearly in the picture without overdoing it (one big logo is often better than lots of little ones).

# Interview tips

If your news release is successful and you secure a radio or television interview, then here are a few tips to help.

# General

### Be prepared but no scripts, no memorised speeches

You should prepare in advance, making sure you know as much as possible about the topic for your interview. However, if you do not know something be willing to say so. It is better to do this than get something wrong.

Do not use a script. However, it is acceptable to have documents to hand if there is a very complicated statistic or a quote you want to give accurately. You need to be able to turn immediately to the relevant place. In most cases you will know far more than the person interviewing you, particularly if this is at a local level. Generally, interviewers are prompting you to get the best out of the interview. Even the national journalists with a reputation for grilling their guests are willing you to come up with an answer so that they can help the audience understand the issues.

## Think about the best person for the interview

Development workers, project managers and volunteers working at grassroots level can sometimes be more interesting interviewees than the 'suits' at one remove from what is taking place. Think about whom you are offering for interview and what they will have to offer the interviewer. Policy and strategy can sound dry and dull. Passion, commitment and down-to-earth examples are easier for listeners and viewers to understand.

## Approach an interview with enthusiasm

If you participate in an interview with energy and enthusiasm then the audience will pay attention. It does not matter if in your enthusiasm you stumble over a word or two. The overall impression will be of someone who cares about their cause. If you become over-anxious, stiff and formal it makes the audience nervous too and keen to tune in to someone else.

## Cut out the jargon

Before the interview think about some of the most difficult concepts that you have to express. Try to put these ideas into simple everyday terms, perhaps drawing on examples or comparisons. Imagine explaining the point to an aunt or uncle, because they will be in the programme's audience.

## Consider the questions

You will go into the interview knowing that you have one key message to get across. Do not just blurt it out after the first question. It can get the whole interview off to a bad start and sounds stilted. If your message naturally forms part of your answer to the first question, fine. But do not force it.

Most interviewers will ask you beforehand if there is anything in particular you want to say or be asked. Some will give you a general opening at the end. If you really feel the opportunity is going to slip away, you could reply to a final question with, 'That's a really interesting question, but at the moment we're focusing on . . .' or, 'That's a good point, but we find that there is an even greater problem with . . .'

### Remain open to other views

If you are campaigning on a controversial issue then you might find yourself interviewed alongside someone with opposing views. Even if the other person is rude, ignorant and arrogant, try to keep cool. If you can maintain a calm and polite approach you will retain your dignity while they appear childish. Do not try to score points. Be open and listen to their views and then respond. Start by acknowledging the other person and their right to their opinions. Then indicate you have considered the matter and made your decision on solid ground. You might say something along the lines of, 'I understand your point of view John, but we've talked to 1,000 people directly affected by X. Our research shows overwhelmingly that . . .'

# Radio

### Down the line

Local and national radio stations increasingly conduct interviews over the phone, preferring an ISDN line but perfectly happy with a normal office or home telephone connection. In one sense such interviews are less nerve racking because you do not have to deal with the paraphernalia of microphones and the atmosphere of the studio. On the other hand such interviews can be disconcerting because you cannot see the interviewer to gain visual clues as to how the interview is going. You do not have any real preliminary chat.

### Short and sharp

Commercial radio rarely uses more than a soundbite from an interview. This is another reason to avoid jargon, and to be energetic in your approach. Smile as you speak; it really does come over on radio. If you are on local radio try to relate what you are saying to the local area.

For instance, if you have just received funding for something do not simply say, 'We're thrilled. We've worked so hard for this money and it is great for our organisation. Now we can employ two more development workers and re-equip our offices.' Instead say something like, 'We're thrilled. We've worked so hard for this money and now our organisation can help three times as many people in Southampton. We hope to find supported employment for 300 people in the city each year.' Local radio reporters like to show how the news relates specifically to people living, and listening, in their area.

### Be available

If you really want to be interviewed then sometimes you need to be available at odd times. Sometimes there is little flexibility and it is either come in to the studio, or do a down-the-line, at this time or not at all. Often this means early in the morning (during the breakfast/drive-time slot) or at a weekend. If you want the interview you need to be prepared for unsocial hours.

An arts organisation sent out news releases about a forthcoming campaign to highlight the importance of arts work with young people. A London radio station wanted an interview and the relevant person refused to speak to them at their only available time – because she was going to have her hair done. Luckily they had someone else who could speak equally authoritatively on the subject who was a little more flexible (and perhaps a little more confident too).

# Television

## Think visually

Think about what you might be able to provide that is of visual interest. You might have something going on that is so visually interesting that this alone will tempt a television news crew along. For instance, if you have a record-breaking human pyramid, built out of people standing on each other's shoulders, this would make a great photo. But it also makes a good piece of tele as people talk ambitiously beforehand and as a nervous wobble adds to the tension.

## Dress appropriately

If you are promoting a grassroots piece of development work, do not don a pin-stripe suit for the cameras if you do not normally wear one. Dress to feel comfortable and to fit in with the environment. If you are a sports worker who normally wears a tracksuit, this will look fine on television, and will help to get your logo on camera. It adds to the atmosphere and will make you look relaxed. Bright white, checks and elaborate patterns cause camera problems, so avoid them if possible.

## Set aside sufficient time

Filming for television takes time. Unless something is being broadcast live there is a very high ratio of material filmed compared to that which is transmitted. A crew could be with you for two hours to get a minute for the news. If you are feeling stressed about the time being taken then you will not give the best interview. So, be prepared and set aside more time than you think will be needed.

# Advertising

So far we have talked about securing editorial coverage for your cause. You can also pay for space and advertise. The downside is the cost unless you can work together with a sponsoring body who will run a joint campaign.

# Newspaper advertising

There are different advertising rates depending on where in the paper you place your ad. If you want an advert on the main editorial pages it is more expensive than putting an ad in the classified section. The more prominent the news pages the more expensive the ad, and the bigger the circulation the more expensive the rates.

You may not be used to putting a promotional ad into a newspaper, but you probably use newspapers to recruit new staff. Next time you are advertising a job, think about how you can also promote your organisation to a wider audience too. It might be that you include an extra line of copy or word the advert slightly differently to highlight a specific campaign.

If you buy space to run a fundraising or campaigning advert, here are some points to consider.

### Use active 'doing' words

Instead of saying, 'School friends charity desperate for cash,' say, 'Buy a brick and help us build our new classroom.' Write your advert from the point of view of the reader – how they can help. Do not just tell them about your situation.

### Draw the reader in with a bold gripping heading

It adds to the space and cost, but go for a big bold heading. There is no point in buying an ad that people do not notice. The words you use need to draw people in: you could intrigue them, shock them, tease them. The heading is one of the most important parts of the ad so spend time on it with colleagues. Test it out with people first. If they do not respond do not take it personally. The constructive criticism will help you spend your money wisely.

### Let the advert 'breathe'

Do not cram in so much copy that the advert ends up looking too daunting to read. Include white space and the advert is much more appealing.

### Include an easy response mechanism

You want people to take action as a result of the ad, so make it easy for them. You might include something that they can cut out and return (encouraging them by offering a freebie perhaps, or by running a competition). Be sure to include contact details, including web and e-mail addresses as well as phone, fax and text phone numbers.

### Tell them what their involvement will mean

Do not just invite them to take part; quantify their involvement. If you are asking for money say what £5 or £10 will 'buy'. If you are asking for their action say what this means for the project and make it seem easy: an hour of their time, one more signature on a petition, a Saturday morning each month.

### Include a quote from a beneficiary

An appeal directly from the person who will benefit can motivate people to take action.

# Radio advertising

Radio advertising is quite a cost-effective option for local campaigns and you might be able to negotiate a discount because of the nature of your campaign. The advert, or adverts, will probably be around 30 seconds long. It is sufficient time for you to state your case, include some 'actuality' or sound from real life and an invitation to take part. If you are giving a phone number you will want to give a reminder so it is given out at least twice in the ad. The radio station will either produce the ads for you or recommend an agency.

# Television and cinema advertising

A few charities have worked successfully with commercial sponsors or with advertising agencies offering their services free of charge to develop TV and cinema advertising campaigns. If you are in this position then you will be working with some highly creative people who know how to engage people's emotion and translate interest into action. The important role you have, though, is to:

- explain exactly what you want to achieve;
- ensure the proposed advert conveys the right image for your organisation;
- ensure the advert gets across the right messages;
- be a critical friend during the production process, to help the agency get it right;

- be a spokesperson in any accompanying media campaign to draw attention to your adverts;
- ensure you have all the back-up in place to handle a response to the campaign.

# Main stages in communicating via the media

### Agree your message and target audience

Define what it is that you are trying to say and who you want to reach. This is essential to help you decide on the right approach.

### Devise a PR/advertising plan

Work out how you will get the media interested in your campaign. Draw up a timetable that includes both editorial input and, if appropriate, advertising. If you are using both then they should complement each other.

### Agree a budget

See below for suggestions as to what should go into the budget.

### Ensure response mechanisms are in place

You need to be able to handle the enquiries generated by your campaign.

### Put the plan into action

You may need to be 'available' 24 hours a day at the start of the campaign, so clear your diary if you are doing something on a large scale.

# Setting a budget

### Person time

At the very least you, or a colleague, will be spending time drafting news releases, making contact with journalists and providing interviews. This can be costed into a PR budget.

### Materials

You may have exhibition boards, branded merchandise and logo banners readily available. If not, you may want to create some to feature in photo opportunities. We give more detail on this in the following chapters.

## Photography

You cannot always expect the press to turn up at events. If you want to ensure you have a good shot to issue afterwards, then you might want to commission a professional photographer.

## Agencies

If you are placing an advert you might want a graphic design company to lay it out for you; you might use an agency to create a radio ad.

## Advertising space

Ring up for an advertising pack to find out the general prices for advertising. Then speak to an individual and negotiate a deal that you can afford.

## Other expenses

If you are putting on a launch event then you will need to budget for refreshments and maybe room hire, audio-visual (AV) equipment, and other event costs.

# 7

# Open days, roadshows, balls, conferences and exhibitions

So far in this book we have talked about promoting your cause to a wide audience through different long-distance means. In the next two chapters we look at some of the opportunities presented by face-to-face activities. This section focuses on events that people drop in to. It is up to you to come up with an event that highlights the importance of your work. The communication is pretty much one-to-one.

**After reading this chapter you will have ideas on:**

▶ how to organise an effective event;
▶ developing eye-catching display materials;
▶ ensuring people turn up to your event.

## Words of advice

There are three important phrases to bear in mind if you want to organise a brilliant event. They are:

### 'Attention to detail'

You have ordered cloths for the tables, which is good, but not good enough. Do you know what colour the cloths will be? Do you know the size of the tables? Have you ordered flowers for the tables? What type and colour will they be? When you think you have got everything sorted, run through your plan and ask such questions at every stage. This attention to detail is what makes the difference between an event that is quite good, where occasionally you have to cobble things together to get through, and one that runs smoothly.

After a few events with this kind of questioning beforehand you almost develop a new 'event-planning' sense. Something will be nagging at the back of your mind until you run through the itinerary. Then it will hit you: you have ordered flipcharts but you have not ordered pens or paper.

Do not leave anything to chance.

## 'Assumption is the mother of all cock-ups'

One of your colleagues always seems to turn up an hour before an event begins. Do not assume they are going to do so on this occasion. Give them a schedule and ask them if they can arrive at this time. Otherwise, this will be the first time they turn up at the start time and you are left short-staffed for getting everything ready. The really devastating assumption is the one where because someone says they will do something you assume that they do. Check that they have done so, ask for details. Otherwise you could be let down at the last minute.

## 'If it can go wrong it will go wrong'

Have contingency plans in place. For instance, pay a technician to be on hand for if (when?) the PowerPoint presentation goes pear-shaped or for when the microphones start to whistle.

# Different kinds of events

With these key points in mind, let us look at some of the events you might organise to help promote your cause.

## Open days

Open days sound like you simply throw open the doors and give people the chance to drop by. However, if they are to be successful there is much more involved. For a start you need to tell people in plenty of time so that they put the date in the diary. You also need to make the event sufficiently interesting for them then to bother to turn up. You need to ensure that key workers do not go off on leave for the day. You should also give some people roles during the day such as putting them in charge of welcoming guests, showing them round, explaining particular projects.

You might want to organise an open day for people who have supported your organisation in the past and for your current funders. Include individual donors, local authorities, government agencies, lottery distributors, companies and trusts. You are offering them a good opportunity to see that they have invested wisely, to network with others and appreciate your hospitality. You have a great opportunity to make people feel good so that they pro-actively offer more help or are well disposed to your approach on a later date.

You could hold an open day for current supporters and ask them to bring along friends and family who do not know much about your campaign. Use the opportunity to show them a little of your organisation and your work. As an incentive, include a meal or children's fun day. It is an opportunity to thank your supporters for their efforts, to thank your supporters' friends and family for putting up with the time away from them, and to recruit new supporters.

# Roadshows

You cannot always entice people to your events. Sometimes you have to go to them. A roadshow is about dropping in on people when they are out shopping, relaxing or travelling. You go to a place with a lot of people passing through and try to interest them in your work.

A lot of pre-planning is involved. Even if you are not doing direct fundraising, there will still be a lot of permissions needed before you can pitch up with your stall. Some supermarket foyers have three-month waiting lists.

One of the advantages of a roadshow is the number of people you can reach in a short space of time. If you run a series of events over a week you could reasonably expect to talk to at least 1,000 people. You get the chance to put your message face-to-face with complete strangers who may have not even considered supporting your campaign before they meet you. It is hard work. People often assume you are going to try to sell them a conservatory. So use free gifts to attract them over: balloons for children, free pens, badges, stickers. Once they are over by your table or exhibition you can start to chat. Try to get people's names and addresses so that you can send them further information; you might run a prize draw, for instance.

Roadshows are extremely hard work. Wear comfortable shoes.

# Balls

Fundraising dinners or balls are complex to organise and can be very stressful for the coordinator as you are often taking quite large risks in predicting ticket sales. If you can persuade a sponsor to under-write the event then you will get many more peaceful nights' sleep and your trustees will probably be happier too. The advantage of balls are that they are extremely enjoyable for the participants: they give money and at the same time get real, almost instant pleasure from the donation. People are in a receptive mood when you put across your key messages through after-dinner speeches, programmes and so on. Balls have a glitzy image and so you need to think about how this fits with your work.

## Conferences

Like balls conferences often involve an element of risk as you book venues, food and printing all before you have sold a single place. Yet, they are a great way to raise awareness. You can make a modest amount of funds, but essentially conferences are about learning, sharing and networking.

Conference organisation is very labour intensive. Most delegates respond in the three or four weeks before the event, some the day before, and the odd one or two on the day itself. Presenters leave their AV arrangements until the last possible moment and every one will have different AV requirements. Just before the event there are 200 packs to stuff with 50 different leaflets, signs to prepare for every doorway in the venue, and 101 last minute details to finalise with the venue. On the day people are needed on registration, to direct people to rooms, to hold microphones in the audience; the list can be endless.

## Exhibitions

Many of us are familiar with exhibiting at shows put on by other agencies, but have you considered putting on an exhibition of your own? You may charge other organisations a small fee to take part. Together you have a range of stands on a similar theme, offering people the chance to find out more in a fairly comprehensive way.

A campaigner who wanted to raise awareness of visual impairment organised an exhibition called 'Different viewpoints'. Her own organisation is a charity whose members are blind or partially sighted. The group works closely with social services, an independent living centre, neighbouring associations for blind people, a sports centre and an arts venue. They put on a joint exhibition which included resources, computer software demonstrations, and poetry.

Of those who attended 60% were blind or partially sighted, yet only 20% were connected with the organisations represented. A further 30% had a friend or relative with a significant visual impairment. The remaining 10% dropped in because the exhibition 'sounded interesting'.

# Planning your event

You need a project plan for your event so that you are clear about the aims and objectives, the timetable and how to judge whether or not it was successful. Ideally begin planning your event a good three to six months beforehand. If you are organising a high profile fundraising event then it is best to work on it over at least a 12-month period.

Event committees can be very supportive but they can also be a brake on progress. If you are working with a committee be clear about its role and agree at the outset on decisions that can be taken between meetings by the event coordinator.

If there is any kind of charge for your event then it is important to agree a firm rule on who, if anyone, is eligible for free or subsidised places. To help the discussion you can focus first on general guests. However, it is important to be clear about how this might apply to people on the committee, trustees, session leaders, volunteers and so on. Time and again event budgets are thrown into disarray because of the number of free places claimed by people involved with the event organisation.

Schedule regular reviews of progress, and a date when you formally decide whether or not the event should take place. Take out relevant insurance and make sure you have the permissions you need from the various authorities. Write everything down, including telephone conversations. It all seems clear and simple at the time, but events build up layer by layer. You will find your notebook invaluable.

# Exhibition panels and materials

There are a number of promotional items that you might want for events (in addition to your literature) including the following.

## Exhibition panels

There are various options to choose from. You can go for felt-style boards to which you attach panels with velcro. You can get table-top versions, sets with four squares over four, free-standing boards, interlocking boards and so on. In addition to the velcro panels you can also get ones with magnetic strips that attach to an expandable mesh. Freestanding sails are also increasingly used because they are so versatile and portable. After design, each one costs approximately £500 to produce including the printing.

## Leaflet display

Simple leaflet racks are available from office supply companies, but if you want exhibition shelving, or an integrated desk and display then you will need to talk to an exhibition specialist. They can custom-build to your requirements (at a price, of course).

## TV or computer monitor

You might invest in a TV with integrated video or DVD to form part of your exhibition. You might want to use a computer demonstration too.

## What to include in your display panels

Large high quality photographs make a big impact in a display. Accompany them with some explanatory text. Graphics work well on a large scale, such as to illustrate plans for a building or graphs to show the impact of a project. Do not assume that all of your text has to be big enough for people to read at a distance. People normally walk to and fro, standing back and peering closely.

## Encouraging interactivity

If you want feedback, comments, ideas and suggestions you could incorporate things such as a graffiti panel/wall (you might want to check this regularly); a suggestions box; or a computer message board.

# Attracting interest

You might put together the most meticulous event, but it is wasted effort if no one turns up. What, then, can you do to attract interest and how can you ensure people come along?

Here are some suggestions.

## Involve your target audience in designing the event

If you want to make sure that your event is going to attract your target audience, consult some of them when you are planning the event. Ask them to tell you what they want from such an occasion.

## Use people to reach people

Asking one person to get 100 people to an event is giving them a tough job. Inviting 10 people to bring along 10 friends or colleagues is much easier. Getting 20 people to invite five friends is even more achievable.

### Promote your event with flyers, posters and media coverage

Face-to-face invitations are highly successful. By contrast between three and ten per cent of flyers will normally lead to bookings. The response to media coverage varies with the prominence and size of any articles.

### Approach key people with personal invitations and phone calls

The personal approach is highly productive. You cannot do it with everyone, but you can target those whom you definitely want to attend.

### Use e-mail to keep people informed

Once people have booked you want to retain their interest. Sending a confirmation letter is a good idea but you cannot keep on posting things to them. However, with e-mail you can write to them a couple more times without it seeming like over-kill. Keeping the event in their mind means they are more likely to turn up.

### Write in the week before the event

Send a map or further piece of written correspondence in the week before the event. This is a reminder to attend. It is a chance to reinforce the benefits they will get from attending and to mention factors like the number and type of other people coming along.

# Stages in preparing for an event

Here are some of the stages you might go through in preparing for an event.

- Come up with an event plan, covering aims, objectives, timetable, marketing and so on.
- Outline key personnel involved, and assign tasks or roles both in the run up to the event and on the day itself.
- Form an event committee with clearly defined roles.
- Sort out insurance and any legal issues, e.g. light entertainment licence.
- Book speakers, workshop leaders, celebrities, VIPs and others.
- Find and hire venue, provide briefs of anticipated AV requirements, room layouts, numbers for catering, and refreshments required.
- Develop promotional literature and draw up list of organisations/individuals to target.
- Brief those involved in marketing and begin promoting the event.
- Have response mechanism in place to handle bookings.
- Send out confirmations and keep people updated through e-mail.

- Meet to decide whether or not the event is to go ahead in the light of bookings.
- Confirm numbers and more detailed arrangements with the venue.
- Send further information/reminder to participants.
- Brief people who will have a role on the day.
- Prepare all materials to distribute and display.
- Be prepared for almost anything to go wrong.
- Evaluate and write a report after the event.

# Setting a budget

Your event budget will probably have the following lines in it:

## Management time

You may commission an external agency to prepare and coordinate the event for you, but there will still be a certain amount of your own time involved in liaising.

## Venue costs

The venue might be self contained and have technicians, caterers, AV equipment and so on. Alternatively you may simply be paying for the room space and for the chairs to be set out in a U-shape.

## Catering

Whether the venue offers this or you need to buy in a caterer, you need a line in the budget for refreshments. There will normally be a variety of menus to choose from depending on how much you are prepared to spend.

## Audio-visual

Many conference venues have most AV equipment and offer this for a small extra fee. Some equipment may have to be hired in. Technician time is almost always an extra charge.

## Promotion

You need to cover the cost of printing flyers, mailings and other promotional materials.

## Access

You need to ensure that anyone who wants to attend is not prevented from doing so because of disability, language, childcare or other access issues. Put a line in the budget to pay for support costs as necessary.

### Transport and travel

This covers your costs, but in addition put a line in for contributors' expenses. If you invite someone to speak it is normal courtesy to pay their travel costs if not a fee.

### Free places

If you are charging for places and expect to give some away for free, put a line in the budget. Then it is clear just how many are available.

### Bursaries

To ensure people are not prevented from attending because they are on a low income, offer a bursary fund.

### Contingency

Something inevitably crops up that you had not thought of. Include a 10% contingency if possible.

For more about events, see *Organising Special Events* (see *Further information* on p110).

# 8

# Making a presentation

You can almost become the 'face' of an organisation for the hundreds of people you speak to. You need to ensure you are giving the right messages about your group and the work it does.

**In this chapter we cover how to:**

▶ prepare by finding out about the context of your presentation;

▶ structure a presentation;

▶ deliver your message effectively;

▶ encourage interaction;

▶ use supporting materials successfully.

## Knowing the context of your presentation

Before you can come up with a presentation you need as much information as possible about whom you will be speaking to and in what context. Hopefully, whoever is organising the event will provide briefing notes. If they do not then here are some of the things you need to know.

## Who will be in the audience?

How many people are expected to attend your presentation? Who are they? What kinds of organisations do they represent and what position do they hold in that organisation? Is it possible to have a list of names beforehand? All of this information will help you to know what sort of content to include and what level to pitch it at.

A human rights campaigner delivered a presentation to 200 academics in quite a formal lecture setting. She knew who would be in the audience and what was expected of her and prepared a lecture on comparing different countries' definitions of 'human rights'. What no one had told her was that a third of the audience came from Spanish-speaking countries and they were sat in small groups with a translator (live audio interpretation was not available). This meant that she had to slow the pace of her presentation slightly, causing her to over-run her slot by 10 minutes.

## What is the venue like?

You might be speaking at an open air rally, in a formal lecture theatre, in a comfortable conference centre, in an airless committee room, in a village hall or in a religious building. Find out what you can about the overall space in which you will be speaking and the layout of the room. Chairs set out in a U-shape helps the meeting feel friendly and encourages eye contact with delegates, but it is unwieldy with more than about 25 people. However, even with rows of chairs it is good to give them a slightly curved shape to draw people in. Try to visualise yourself in this space; it will help you to feel confident about your presentation.

An environmental fundraiser was invited to make a presentation to a group of local authorities about his project, explaining how it was possible to work in partnership. He was so excited about the opportunity to raise awareness and possibly interest councils in contributing financially that he failed to ask about the venue.

One of the coordinators met him at the station and told him the meeting was in progress and if they hurried he could make his presentation before lunch. They arrived at a large civic centre, entered a magnificent old hall and the fundraiser found himself in front of an audience of 100. He did not even have any time to take his notes out of his briefcase before he was invited to make his presentation. He admits it did not go well largely because he just was not expecting an audience of that size nor that kind of imposing venue.

## What is the rest of the event about?

What is the event called and what has been said about it to those coming along? If you are one of a number of speakers, what is everyone else talking about? If you know what the aim of the event is then this is the starting point for your presentation. For example, if the overall aim of the event is to inform community development workers of the value of sport in tackling social exclusion you know to focus on your sporting inclusion project, rather than your arts inclusion project. If the overall aim is to share good practice in drugs education you know to highlight the things that have worked and the things that have not worked so well. You might want to get in touch with other speakers to find out what they will be talking about to avoid duplication and to help you get the right tone with your presentation.

## What am I expected to speak about?

Is there a programme for the event? If so are you listed in it? What does it say you are going to speak about? People expect the presentation that is advertised so make sure you know what has been said about you.

## Where do I come in the schedule?

Finally, find out how your slot relates to the rest of the programme. Perhaps you are giving a talk after a piece of entertainment, after a meal or before a celebrity. Knowing where you come in the programme can help you anticipate the mood of the audience. You might be able to slip in a little appropriate humour to get the audience on your side.

# Structuring a presentation

There is no formula for the perfect presentation though there are some rules that can help you with your first few. Below we suggestion some ideas on how to structure your presentation.

## Good beginnings

Before you start your formal presentation, begin with an informal anecdote or comment. It is amazing the number of good speakers who will begin with 'I was on the way here today when . . .' stories. What these are designed to do is again help everyone to relax. The presenter is showing their human side; they are showing they have a sense of humour and they are making a personal connection with the audience. If the audience has warmed to you as a person before you begin then you should get a good response from them throughout.

If anecdotes just do not come naturally to you, then try a show of hands. This is another way of establishing a bit of a rapport with the audience. Ask how many people have done something that is relevant to your presentation. Another alternative is a poem or creative writing extract. In fact a poem can be used to open or close a presentation. A poem engages the audience's emotions and can help set the scene or send people off feeling differently.

## Now, what are you going to say?

- Tell them what you are going to tell them.
- Tell them.
- Tell them what you have told them.

It is almost a cliché but this really is at the heart of a good presentation. You explain what you are going to cover in your presentation. You run through your presentation. Then you highlight the key points that you have included.

It can seem a bit artificial to approach a presentation in this way, but it certainly helps to distinguish your presentation from a general chat. The good things about this approach are:

- You really do feel that you are giving a presentation. Take a breath and say, 'Today I'm going to talk to you about . . .' You are in charge. You know what you are going to say. It should help you feel confident.
- The audience knows what to expect. You are not going to ramble on for hours. You are not going to talk about something irrelevant. You are not going to talk about something they do not understand. They relax and feel confident.
- You are forced to follow your structure. If you have promised to cover a number of points, then you need to deliver the goods. You cannot go off at a tangent for too long.

## Think in threes

If you want people to take in what you are saying, then ideally make three main points and elaborate on these three themes. If you present more than three key ideas then although the audience may follow you at the time, they will find them hard to remember afterwards.

If you are making a presentation to potential funders take along a full written proposal. Explain that this provides a detailed outline of your project, but that you want to take this opportunity to cover three crucial areas: the need for your project; how you intend to address this need; how your project meets the funder's priorities. If you successfully establish these three points then you are well on the way to convincing the funder to support you. If you go into explanations of aims and objectives, timetables, evaluation and so on, the audience will find it difficult to keep paying attention.

If you are making a presentation to key decision makers then take along supporting documents such as research findings and campaign ideas. Refer the audience to these for further information, but explain that you want to focus on three important points: the problem or need; how you propose to tackle these issues; how the audience can help from their point of view. First you get them to care about the issue, then you show that things can be changed with positive action, and finally you tell them how they can make a difference themselves.

## Get personal at the end

Throughout the presentation you may use anecdotes to bring the talk to life. A personal story at the end is very effective indeed. You might talk about yourself or you might give a powerful example of an individual who has been touched by your work.

This is the one occasion where you should not tell the audience too much about what is coming. Perhaps just begin: 'Before I close let me tell you about Timmy. Timmy has no brothers or sisters. Timmy has no mother or father. All of Timmy's relatives were killed last year . . .' The audience will end up knowing how your work is going to make life better for at least one individual, and hopefully, they will want to help too.

# Delivering your presentation with confidence

How do you feel when someone invites you to give a presentation? Are you thrilled at the opportunity to get your message across to a large number of people in one go? Or do you worry from now until after it is all over? It is quite natural to feel nervous beforehand, and to a certain extent this helps. It means you spend more time preparing than you might do if you approached it in a casual way. It also means you have some nervous energy which can be harnessed to make your presentation lively and a little larger-than-life.

So look on your nerves as making a positive contribution to your presentation. Then also use some of the following techniques to help you build your confidence.

## Think about what you know

You will probably know far more about your specialist area than anyone else in the audience. That puts you in a position of power. If you know less than your audience about something then be honest about this. Say you want to raise questions through your presentation and chair a discussion afterwards. You should never be in a position of giving a presentation where you are bluffing about your level of knowledge. This will not give you confidence and you could easily be thrown off balance by an informed question from the audience.

## Use prompt cards

You might like to write a presentation out in full to begin with, but you should never work from a complete script at the event. Unless you are a professional broadcaster you end up sounding like a robot. The monotone really does send people to sleep. You need to make eye contact with your audience. You need to be animated. This is simply impossible if you have to read out every word. Use prompt cards instead with bullet points. You can move around with them, look people in the eye, and sound spontaneous. Your presentation may be different every time you deliver it but it will benefit from this.

## Tape yourself

Record your presentation onto audio tape and then play this in the car. It will help you to remember key sections of the presentation. You can also decide if some things need to be approached in a different way.

## Use props

You do not have to use sophisticated AV aids to make a good presentation (although we talk about these below). In fact if you are feeling a bit worried about your presentation it makes sense to avoid PowerPoint presentations, live web demonstrations and the like. Stay focused on your presentation. This does not stop you using everyday objects as props. You might hold up a globe and point out all the areas in the world where your organisation works. You might hold up a piece of art or craft work made by one of your service users. You might bring on a box with three items inside, one for each of the themes you are talking about. It all helps to carry the presentation forward and retain the audience's interest. And it gives you power: you know why you have brought the box on stage, you now what is in it.

## Keep doing it and enjoy it

There is no doubt that the first few times you make a presentation it is extremely nerve racking. If you keep making presentations and are prepared to learn from what goes down well and what does not, then you should get better. And as you get better you gain in confidence.

# Encouraging interaction

One way of enlivening your presentation and ensuring the audience are paying attention is to encourage some kind of interaction. Just how actively they can become involved will depend on the numbers in the audience and the physical constraints of the venue. Here are some of the ways in which your presentation can become two-way.

## Show of hands

We have already mentioned this as a way of kicking off your presentation. If the audience are not already warmed up you might need to ask a really silly question to start off with to get them laughing and participating. Then you can ask more serious questions.

## Vote with their feet

If there are 50 or fewer people and you are in a fairly large space you can get people out of their seats to express their views. You can ask them to stand somewhere along a line to show how strongly they agree or disagree with a statement. You can get them to form groups in different corners of the room depending on the type of organisation they represent or the kind of work they do. As with the show of hands this is something that you can do at the beginning of a presentation to engage the audience from the outset.

## The magician's assistant

'Right, I'd like to invite someone from the audience to help me with a demonstration.' It is a technique used successfully in entertainment, and you can use it in a presentation. It is an unusual approach and you need to be able to keep chatting whilst your volunteer helps to demonstrate something such as the impossibility of being in three places at once.

A fundraiser for an environmental charity working with a group of learning disabled adults wanted to raise money for a paper shredder. The idea was that with a shredder the group could transform old newspapers into horse bedding. At an environmental forum attended by council officers, the voluntary sector and local business the fundraiser invited a volunteer on stage. The volunteer was given a pile of newspapers and asked to shred them whilst the fundraiser continued with her presentation. Five minutes later the fundraiser asked for the shredded material, which was sufficient for the hamster cage she had with her. 'Now you can see why, if we're to shred enough material for horses, we need a mechanical shredder!' she said. It was an entertaining presentation and the point was well made.

## Questions and answers

The more traditional way of getting interactive with your audience is to open the presentation up to questions and answers. If you genuinely want to encourage questions then do not say, 'Has anyone got any questions?' Say, 'Who wants to ask the first question?' After you have answered each one, to encourage more questions say something like, 'That was a really good question. Who has another question on that topic?' Do not be afraid to admit you do not know the answer to a question; instead, offer to find out the answer and take the enquirer's details.

## Presentation aids

There are a number of presentation aids you can use to support your talk and we run through them below, with a few hints about how to get the best out of them.

## Flipcharts

The most basic presentation aid is a flipchart. If you are working with a small group of up to 30 people, then a flipchart is a great tool. It encourages you to move around, to ask the audience for contributions and capture the essential points to come out of the meeting. You can pre-prepare some of the flipchart sheets so that they are nice and neat, but this makes the presentation less dynamic and really the flipchart ends up acting like a low-tech overhead projector (OHP).

# Overhead projectors

OHPs can be used successfully with groups of up to 100 or so people. The downside to OHPs is that the hairs and scratches on the projector can make the projected image look scrappy. The upside is that they are so flexible, you can mix and match OHP sheets depending on your particular audience. You can add something at the last minute without any hassle.

If you are using an OHP and you are not supplying the equipment, then arrive in plenty of time to see what has been provided. Test out some of your OHPs to ensure the projector is positioned correctly and the screen can be read from the back of the room.

A splash of colour makes OHP presentations look much better. But again make sure you test out your OHP sheets in case some of the colours do not project well. Use strong colours to highlight certain things, but stick to black or dark strong colours like green, purple or blue for the main writing.

# Slides

Glass-mounted 35mm slides project well, giving high quality images with a lot of detail. You need to spend time getting them into the appropriate order and keep good notes as to what you have put into a slide carousel if you are not to get muddled in the middle of your presentation. Do test them out beforehand because it is very embarrassing if your most important slide is projected upside down.

> A keynote speaker at a conference on child poverty began his presentation with a series of slides depicting stunning paintings, architecture and sculpture 'because they are simply so beautiful that I wanted to share them with you. I also wanted to show the very best that we humans are capable of producing before I give a presentation on some of the worst aspects of human nature.'

# Video

Short bursts of video (five to ten minutes) can make a valuable contribution to a presentation, provided they are directly relevant. To get the best effect they should be back-projected onto a large screen rather than shown on a TV monitor (unless the audience numbers around 20 or so).

## Data projection

PowerPoint presentations are increasingly popular and when they work well they can look professional and add information effectively. Used badly they are a distraction, and when the technology fails they can be a disaster. As well as using data projection for PowerPoint presentations, you can also project websites and little animations using the same technology as is used on websites (Flash).

Here are a few tips on how to make your PowerPoint presentation work well:
- Incorporate your logo in a subtle way (so that it does not distract from the main information on the screen).
- Use subtle shades for the background, reflecting and complementing the colours in your logo.
- Use dark colours or black for the main text so that it is easy to read.
- Do not cram too much information onto a single screen. Generally the number of bullet points allowed in the slide templates are the maximum you should use.
- Incorporate pictures or graphics to illustrate points, rather than just listing the main things you are saying.
- Use one or two different methods of transition between screens. You are given many different options: wipes from left and right, up and down, dissolves, checkerboard, fades and so on. If you use too many it just looks like you have got carried away with the technology. Use one or two and the simplicity gives coherence to the presentation.
- Do not rely on the PowerPoint. Be prepared for the technology to fail or not be available. It can and does go wrong.

PowerPoint gives you a good opportunity to highlight 'before' and 'after' scenarios. You simply create two screens that are laid out in the same way with images of something you want to transform and the images of what you hope to achieve. Then by dissolving from one to the other the audience can see what a difference their support can make. As well as using images of people and places you can do something similar with bar charts and other graphs.

## Stages in preparing for a presentation

If you are invited to make a presentation, here are the main stages in preparing for the event:

### Research

Find out as much as possible about the audience, event, venue, other speakers, overall context.

### Brief

Ask for a brief from the organisers, or find out how you are being 'advertised' to the audience. What do they expect from you?

### Draft presentation

Make a note of the key points you want to get over and then start to structure your presentation. Practice it in full to see if you are working roughly to the available time slot. Prepare prompt cards.

### Audio visual

Check what AV support is available and then prepare supporting materials or props. Test them out to ensure everything works. Find out how early you can get to the venue to try things out in situ.

### Mental preparation

Allow yourself time to arrive and prepare. Breathe deeply and use any nerves for energy.

### Delivery

Use prompt cards, supporting materials and so on to give a dynamic presentation, encourage interaction, and feel in a position of power when you have the microphone. You know what is coming next; the audience does not. You know what you are going to ask of them; they do not. Smile, enjoy yourself, and use the opportunity to get over your key messages.

### Feedback

If you want to improve, welcome any feedback. Do not take it as personal criticism. Use it to do even better next time.

# Setting a budget

If you have been invited to speak to a meeting then your travel expenses will probably be covered. Sometimes you will be offered a fee. The main item of expenditure will be supporting materials. You might commission slides, video or a PowerPoint presentation. You need to be confident that you are going to be speaking on a number of occasions about similar matters if you are to spend this sort of money.

# 9

# Merchandise

**W**e have covered the major ways in which you will promote your cause. Now, in the next three chapters we are going to look at a number of ways you can reinforce your message through: merchandise; support packs; and the organisation as a whole.

**This section focuses on merchandise and explains how to:**

▶ be clear about the purpose of merchandise in promoting your cause;

▶ build up a catalogue of merchandise;

▶ commission the production of merchandise.

## The role of merchandise

It seems like a nice idea to have a T-shirt with your organisation's name and logo and a matching corporate mug. But how are you going to use them to promote your cause?

Before you start commissioning fleeces, lapel badges, ties and key fobs, you need to be clear about why you are doing so, how the merchandise will be used to help promote your cause, and whether it is designed to raise revenue directly or indirectly. It costs money to develop merchandise so you will probably need your board's approval before investing. That means that you should prepare a paper outlining how the merchandise will benefit your organisation. Here are some of the ways in which you might use merchandise:

### Awareness raising

The use of T-shirts, banners and balloons at external events and in photo-opportunities can help to raise the public's awareness of your organisation's identity.

### Volunteer motivation

Providing free T-shirts and mugs to volunteers gives them a sense of belonging and value.

### Revenue generation

If you think there is a market in your supporters and volunteers you might create a fundraising catalogue of merchandise.

### Reminder to donors

You want to remain in your donors' consciousness, but you do not want to bombard them with too much literature. A branded pen or mousemat might mean you are seen by them every day at work.

# Building up a catalogue

You will need to decide on your priorities in building up a catalogue of merchandise. It is unlikely you will be able to afford or want to commission everything on the list below at once. But here are some ideas for branded merchandise that might help you promote your cause.

## Clothing

T-shirts, fleeces, ties, baseball caps, socks: these can all be produced with your branding. Most clothing needs to carry a simple subtle logo. T-shirts can carry additional messages and be used more like sandwich boards. They are probably the most useful piece of clothing merchandise for charities and community groups. There are specialist T-shirt printers, often based locally.

## Badges, stickers, bits and bobs

There are specialist badge-making companies, usually listed in the Yellow Pages. They offer a range of shapes and sizes, including small lapel logo badges which look subtle enough to be worn in television interviews. Stickers come in all shapes and sizes too. You can get car or bumper stickers, little stickers to give to people when they make a donation to a house-to-house collection, stickers to go on re-used envelopes (these cut stationery costs, promote your brand, and show you to be environmentally responsible). Key fobs are another handy, fairly low-cost little item that can be branded. You would probably want to sell them rather than give them away because they do not really have a 'freebie' feel to them.

## Mugs

Many organisations commission branded mugs but you need to be clear about who you want to give them to. It is all very well for staff to drink tea and coffee out of them, but they need to be out and about promoting your message. You might give them away at an exhibition, provided you think people will be able to transport them without a breakage. If a school or business has given you support, you might present them to the key members of staff.

## Flags, banners and balloons

These items are useful for exhibitions, but can also be used as merchandise that you make available to other people. Children love flags and balloons. If you are organising a public event or are exhibiting in a public area, offer flags and balloons and you will see your branding all over town. You need to keep messages simple and use bright colours. Banners are useful for dressing up venues where you are speaking, but you might want to make them available to anyone who is raising money or carrying out activities that help to promote your cause.

A fundraising coordinator for a children's hospice commissioned five banners which included the hospice logo and carried the message 'Caring for children, supporting families'. The banners were first used at a turf-cutting ceremony to celebrate the money raised for a new building. They have also been made available to the Friends of the hospice for fundraising events such as fetes, afternoon teas and fun days.

## Office stationery

Pens, mousemats and memo pads can all be produced with your branding. They all offer scope to carry a specific message about your work. Pens and memo pads are particularly good gift items. People always need new pens and memo pads. People do not always need new mousemats, so they make less ideal free gifts and are perhaps better as paid-for items in a catalogue.

## Other items

Almost any item you can imagine can be produced as a branded product. The more common items listed above are the most cost-effective to commission because the companies that make them are producing similar items for other people all the time.

# Stages in the production of merchandise

As we said above, the first thing you need to do is to come up with a rationale for producing your merchandise: know why you are commissioning it and how it will be used. Then you need to decide what products are appropriate, researching the costs involved and the different companies that manufacture the goods. Some companies offer a 'complete solution' and will coordinate the production of any branded item you want, but you usually pay extra for the coordination cost. If you just want a few products then you might be better off approaching the individual manufacturers who specialise in producing pens or T-shirts. Yellow Pages is a good place to start and if there is nothing in your area then you can do some research on the Internet for appropriate companies. They will usually show examples of some of the products they make.

Ask for samples and prices from companies before commissioning work from them. You need to know what you are buying. Find out how artwork needs to be supplied because you will normally have to come up with the design you want, particularly if you want to be consistent. Decide on the message you want to promote and any contact details (phone numbers, web addresses, and so on) before you commission any work. Again, this encourages consistency.

Then agree a budget and ask to sign-off the work before it goes ahead (to ensure your logo has not been distorted in the process). Remember to agree delivery and storage arrangements. One hundred mugs might not sound very many, but when they are boxed up they take up a fair amount of space.

# Setting a budget

Your merchandise budget might include the following items:

### Project management time

There is a fair amount of coordination work involved in making this happen.

### Design and artwork

You might have a design that naturally translates onto banners and balloons, but you usually need to spend time creating something appropriate. This could be done in-house or be commissioned. Either way it takes time and therefore money.

## Production

You may work with one or several companies. Agree terms for payment so that you know when money will be owed. Try to build in a stage so that you see the quality of the goods before you make the final payment.

## Delivery and storage

There are delivery costs involved in transporting the goods to you from the manufacturer, but also in delivering them on to their final destination. Include both in your budget, along with any cost for storage.

# 10

# Creative packages

**T**his brief chapter focuses on some of the packs you might produce to help promote your cause.

**The chapter is designed to give you some ideas on creating:**

▶ membership packs;
▶ schools resource materials;
▶ volunteer fundraiser packs

## Membership packs

If you raise money from individual donors, or if you encourage individuals to sign up to your campaigns then why not provide them with membership packs? Here are a few ideas on creating effective packs for members.

### Adult packs and family packs

You might produce two different kinds of packs: one for adults and one for families. The family pack might contain some fun ideas including quizzes, word searches, activities, posters, stickers.

### Include background information

There is room in a pack to include quite a bit of information about your organisation and cause.

### Include details of other members

Reassure new members that they have made the right decision to support your cause by including messages from other members, particularly celebrities.

### Include gifts and stickers

Members have been kind enough to give you support, give them a little something too. A pen and some stickers will help you further promote your cause, but also feel like a nice gesture to new members.

A childcare fundraiser had already successfully gained sponsorship from a local independent toyshop. He approached the toyshop when developing a pack for members and asked if they would like to be involved in any way. The toyshop agreed to donate vouchers for its store worth £3 each for 300 membership packs.

## Provide information about different types of support

You want members to keep supporting you and to expand the amount of help they give, so include information about what else they can do for the organisation. But be careful with the tone of this document so that it is not too pushy and off-putting. Work with existing members to create something appropriate.

## Include details of staff and projects

Help members to feel part of the organisation by providing contact details for staff and information about specific projects.

# Schools resource materials

Schools resource packs are another way of promoting your cause. You need to take care to develop a pack that has educational value and is objective about your area of work. If you develop a pack of propaganda then it will not be used and it could damage your organisation's reputation if it receives poor reviews in the educational press.

## Work with educational experts

If you are going to develop something of educational relevance that helps teachers deliver the curriculum you need to work with educational experts: teachers, advisers or consultants.

## Identify how the pack supports the curriculum

Be clear about how your resource pack fits with the current curriculum. Does it help teachers deliver citizenship? Will it meet areas of the personal, social and health education curriculum? Can it help a school become a 'Healthy School'? This information should go into any fliers that promote the pack, and should also be highlighted in the materials themselves.

## Highlight the age range

You also need to flag up to teachers the appropriate age range for the activities.

### Include clear instructions

To be sure that the materials are clear and understandable invite a third party to read through them.

### List questions that are raised

Do not just say, 'Discuss this . . .' Spell out specific questions that should be put to the children.

### Consider including activities for staff

If appropriate you might provide developmental activities for staff if your theme covers something that affects the whole school.

### List sources of further information, including websites

Make it easy for a teacher to follow up the issues raised.

## Ensuring the packs get to the right people

With so many demands on teachers' time it can be hard to ensure your material is used. This is why, though, it is so important to involve teachers throughout the development of your materials. If classroom teachers can see a place for the material in their own teaching experience, then others may have room for it too. If you can get some teachers to try the materials out and provide an endorsement this is helpful. Word of mouth works well in education, but this can be a slow process. If you can link in with relevant teacher advisers then this can help. So too can mentions in the educational press and favourable reviews in mainstream media.

Just as with websites you have to promote the very thing – the pack – that is designed to promote your organisation.

## Volunteer fundraiser packs

If you have help with fundraising from a group of volunteers then you might want to provide them with a support pack. This could include:

- **background information:** on both your organisation and your cause so that they are able to answer questions from the public;

- **leaflets for interested people:** that the volunteers can hand out should anyone express particular interest;

- **stickers:** to provide to people who donate money;

- **guidelines:** covering legal matters and also concerning your particular organisation's approach to fundraising;

- **hints:** covering different types of volunteer fundraising activities with tips for success;

- **help:** a number to call for help and advice, out of hours if necessary.

# Developing your packages

The stages in developing these packages are the same as for any printed material, with probably a little more time spent on research and consultation during the production.

# 11

# Finishing touches

Everyone who works for or comes into contact with your organisation is a potential ambassador for the charity and your cause. Your buildings, your vehicles, your events and activities all offer opportunities to promote your cause.

**In this chapter we provide ideas on how to:**

▶ ensure the whole organisation contributes to the promotion of your cause;
▶ make the most of the different opportunities offered by places, objects and people to promote your cause.

## Reinforcing messages across the whole organisation

It really does not do your organisation any good if the person who answers the phone says, 'Sorry, I'm only a temp, I don't know . . .' Even if the receptionist does not know the answer to a question they should be able to refer a caller to the right person or find out the information and ring back. If you are a fundraiser or campaigner then you need to be good at communicating within your own organisation as well as outside. Otherwise people will be put off when they try to get in touch.

When people visit your offices they can pick up messages from posters, noticeboards and other material around the building. They can also pick up leaflets to take away and spread the word.

## Ideas to consider

Here are some of the things you might do to ensure your organisation is giving out the right messages and supporting your efforts to promote your cause.

## Briefings

Provide briefings to staff and volunteers in which you explain the importance of your cause, how you are working to tackle problems and needs, and how you are promoting this work.

## Training

Offer promotional training to staff and volunteers so that they have the skills to support your efforts. You cannot do it all on your own, but you need to ensure others are giving out the same messages. Provide them with the materials to support such work (e.g. presentation aids and notes).

## Posters and notices

Raise the profile of your cause within the organisation's building. Make sure everyone who works with you understands the key messages you are promoting by displaying posters and notices. These displays will also reinforce your message for any visitor to the building.

## Signage

Incorporate slogans and messages into signs round the building. If you share a building and have signs indicating where you are, add a message about your work.

## Leaflet displays

Put leaflets on display in reception. People can browse and take them while they are waiting.

## Answerphone, e-mail and fax

Do not miss a trick. Put a line in your answerphone message about the work you are doing. Incorporate a message in the footer to your e-mail. Add a message onto your fax headers.

## Campaign updates

Keep colleagues up to date with progress. You do not have to keep calling meetings; you could come up with a campaign bulletin board or large graph to show progress. It will ensure colleagues feel involved in what is happening with your work and they will be more willing to try to answer queries if you are not around.

# 12

# Finding out how you are doing

In almost every chapter we have included information on setting a budget for the different ways you can promote your cause. If you want to reach a wide number of people with your key messages, this usually costs money. If you are spending your organisation's funds to raise more funds or to raise awareness you need to justify to trustees that the money is being used wisely. You need a way of evaluating the impact of your work. This will also help you to develop more effective approaches in future.

**After reading this chapter you will have ideas on:**

▶ how to evaluate different aspects of your promotional work;

▶ how to capture new ideas that can be used in future promotional activity.

## The importance of tracking progress

Evaluating the impact of your promotional work can:

• help show that the money invested has been spent effectively;
• justify a request for further budget to continue and extend the work;
• help you refine your work so that it is more effective in the future.

Some of the work that we have described will directly result in something you can quantify (i.e. you can count something like people or money). Other work will be about raising awareness so that people are more receptive when you later ask them for money, time or action. Even though you cannot count people or money coming forward as a result, you can still make some judgements about the value of the work.

Below we run through the different areas we have covered in this book suggesting some of the many ways in which you might evaluate their effectiveness.

# Different methodologies for different promotional tools

### Printed material

- Feedback: invite written feedback on any printed materials such as annual reports and newsletters. You can use questionnaires or simply ask for reactions. Also keep a feedback book for any comments you hear about your letterhead, corporate design and so on.
- Focus groups: if you are thinking about a new design then work with a small group of colleagues and clients to explore ideas.
- Quantifiable results: if you run a campaign that is calling for action, volunteers or funds, then you will have a record of the results. Produce a report that allows you to compare different campaigns.

### Websites

- Include a feedback (graffiti) page for general comments.
- Include an online questionnaire for people new to the site or for regular users.
- Online campaigns will have tangible results. If the web element is part of a wider campaign ensure you track the Internet responses and do not lump them into the overall statistics.

### Audio and video

- If the video is sent out to people include a short written questionnaire (one that can be faxed back or that includes a pre-paid envelope to encourage responses).
- Include a dedicated phone number for further information so that you can trace any enquiries that result. Also track any requests for additional copies.
- Include a question about the material in an evaluation sheet if you use it as part of your presentation.
- Site a feedback box beside your video if you are using it at an exhibition.

### The media

- Build up a cuttings file: ask colleagues to keep an eye out for any articles that appear.
- Keep a record of radio and television interviews and any subsequent enquiries.

### Open days, exhibitions, balls, conferences and roadshows

- Use evaluation sheets: keep them simple and do not let people go home until they have completed one!
- Provide a graffiti wall for more general remarks.

### Presentations

- Ask the event organisers if you can supply an evaluation sheet or can provide a couple of questions for inclusion in theirs.

### Merchandise

- Keep a record of orders and compare different months and years.
- Asses how much money you are making (if you are offering items for sale).

### Creative packages

- Keep a record of orders and compare different months and years.
- Offer a dedicated hotline number so that you know when the packs have generated enquiries.

### Generally

- Ask anyone making a donation or signing up to your campaign for the first time how they heard about the organisation.
- Carry out detailed member surveys: ask questions about the different elements of your promotional work to see what they value.
- If you can afford it, commission a survey into the general public's awareness of your identity and your work.

# Looking ahead

Hopefully the ideas included in this book will help you to promote your cause more effectively. Nothing we have said is about being a spin doctor. It is all about raising the profile of the work that you are doing, sticking to the principles that govern your organisation, harnessing the passion and energy that led to the creation of your organisation in the first place, and promoting the cause that is at the very heart of everything your organisation stands for.

# Further information

The wide scope of this book inevitably means that we have provided a lot of ideas but have not been able to go into great detail. If any of the sections has sparked off an idea that you would like to follow through and you need more help and information, then some of the organisations and publications listed below could help.

## Books

All the titles in this list published by the Directory of Social Change (DSC) are available from DSC Books, 24 Stephenson Way, London NW1 2DP. Call 020 7209 5151 for a free publications list. Prices were correct at time of going to press but may be subject to change.

**The DIY Guide to Charity Newsletters: For Charities, Voluntary Organisations and Community Groups**
Chris Wells, DSC, 1996, £10.95

**How to Produce Inspiring Annual Reports: A Guide for Voluntary, Arts and Campaigning Organisations**
Ken Burnett and Karin Weatherup, DSC in association with Burnett Works, 2000, £12.50

**Organising Special Events for Fundraising and Campaigning**
John F Gray and Stephen Elsden, DSC, 2000, £10.95

**Marketing and Creative Handbook**
Published annually, available from:
Suite 5
74 Oak Road
Horfield
Bristol BS7 8RZ
Tel: 0117 944 6144
www.mch.co.uk

**Radio Authority Pocket Book**
Radio Authority
Holbrook House
14 Great Queen Street
London WC2B 5DG
Tel: 020 7430 2724
www.radioauthority.org.uk

## Disability access

**British Council of Disabled People (BCODP)**
Litchurch Lane
Litchurch Plaza
Derby DE24 8AA
Tel: 01332 295551
Helpline: 01332 298288
Fax: 01332 295580
Text: 01332 295581
E-mail: general@bcodp.org.uk
www.bcodp.org.uk

**Centre for Accessible Environments (CAE)**
Nutmeg House
60 Gainsford Street
London SE1 2NY
Tel: 020 7357 8182
Fax: 020 7357 8183
Text: 020 7357 8182
E-mail: info@cae.org.uk
www.cae.org.uk

**Council for the Advancement of Communication with Deaf People (CACDP)**
www.cacdp.demon.co.uk

**Disability Rights Commission (DRC)**
FREEPOST
MID 02164
Stratford-upon-Avon CV37 9BR
Tel: 08457 622 633
Text: 08457 622 644
Fax: 08457 778 878
E-mail: enquiry@drc-gb.org
www.drc-gb.org
DRC website links page: www.drc-gb.org/drc/links.asp, which lists various helpful disability organisations.

**Employers' Forum on Disability (EFD)**
Nutmeg House
60 Gainsford Street
London SE1 2NY
Tel/Minicom: 020 7403 3020
Fax: 020 7403 0404
E-mail: efd@employers-forum.co.uk
www.employers-forum.co.uk

**Royal National Institute for Deaf People (RNID)**
19-23 Featherstone Street
London EC1Y 8SL
Tel: 020 7296 8000
Info line: 0808 808 0123
Fax: 020 7296 8199
Text: 0808 808 9000 (Mon-Fri)
E-mail: informationline@rnid.org.uk
www.rnid.org.uk

**Royal National Institute for the Blind (RNIB)**
224 Great Portland Street
London
W1W 5AA
Tel: 020 7388 1266
Helpline: 0845 766 9999
Fax: 020 7388 2034
Text: 0845 758 5691
E-mail: rnib@rnib.org.uk
www.rnib.org.uk

**Youreable**
www.youreable.com

# Magazines

**Broadcast**
33–39 Bowling Green Lane
London EC1R 0DA
Tel: 020 7505 8000
ww.produxion.com

**Creation**
Contentrepublic
3 St Peter's Street
London N1 8JD
Tel: 020 7226 8585
www.365video.com

**Third Sector**
Lime Wharf
Vyner Street
London E2 9DJ
Tel: 020 8709 9050

# Organisations

**BBC**
Television Centre
Wood Lane
London W12 7RJ
Tel: 020 8743 8000
www.bbc.co.uk

**Channel 4 Television**
124 Horseferry Road
London SW1P 2TX
Tel: 020 7396 4444
www.channel4.com

**Independent Television News**
200 Gray's Inn Road
London WC1X 8XZ
Tel: 020 7833 3000
www.itn.co.uk

**Mechanical Copyright Protection Society (MCPS)**
29–33 Berners Street
London W1P 4AA
Tel: 020 8769 4400

**Media Trust**
3–7 Euston Centre
Regent's Place
off Euston Road
London NW1 3JG
Tel: 020 7874 7600
www.mediatrust.org

# Training

The Directory of Social Change runs a variety of courses in the general area of marketing and promotion.

These include:

Marketing for the small organisation
Communicating with conviction
Using the media
Writing effective promotional material

For an up-to-date guide to the training available, call 020 7209 4949 or e-mail training@dsc.org.uk for courses available in London or for information on courses outside London call 0151 708 0117 or e-mail north@dsc.org.uk

# Websites

www.co-financing.co.uk
www.fundraising.co.uk
www.drc-gb.org/drc/links.asp